10 Methoas Of the Heavenly Dragon

One man's encounters with the wonders of the Tao in everyday life.

Line of Intent, Inc. Publishing

London, England

Copyright 2011

This edition published by Line of Intent Books.

Copyright © 2011 by Robert Sheaffer

The moral right of the author has been asserted.

All rights reserved. No part of this publication may be used in any form mechanical or electronic, without prior written permission from Line of Intent Books.

ISBN 978-0-9568186-7-6

All enquires including distribution contact Line of Intent at

retreats108@gmail.com

Cover art detail from "The Gift" by Anna Greaves

Printed and bound by CPI Group (UK) Ltd, Croydon, CRO 4YY

For Dad.

For your gifts of chess and language.

For sharing one hundred with me.

When the superior man hears of the Tao
He diligently practises it
When the average man hears of the Tao
He sometimes holds it and sometimes loses it
When the inferior man hears of the Tao
He laughs aloud at it
If he did not laugh, it would not be the Tao

        Lao Tsu – Tao Te Ching

Foreword

It was on a beautiful summer's evening in Taipei that I first met the Adept that I came to know as Shun Yuan and was able to experience first-hand some of the methods and theories of Taoism and esoteric Buddhism not only being practised in a formal setting but really being lived each and every day.

Shun Yuan is the Adept's name in religion, the name he took when casting off his previous life and committing himself to the pursuit of the Way. The word Yuan means circle or circular and it is the defining characteristic of the art to which this Adept is devoted. Shun has multiple meanings, including connotations of fluidity and a smoothness in the way things go, but also implying submission and following along in compliance with something or other. Over the brief time that I spent with the Adept I was to come to the beginnings of an understanding of that something or other and I hope to be able to share a taste of it here.

When I met him, Shun Yuan refused to allow me to describe him as a Master, choosing instead the term Adept when I enquired what title I should use to refer to him.

"Master," he explained, "indicates that there is a particular relationship between us that likely began as a teacher-student relationship and has grown in depth over time."

Shun Yuan is an itinerant monk of a small sub-sect of Chinese esoteric Buddhism, heavily laced through with Taoist influences, called the Heavenly Dragon Sect and was on an apparently endless peregrination when I encountered him during a temporary pause in his wandering as he spent time in Taipei visiting friends, teaching lessons and of course, drinking copious amounts of Chinese tea.

I realized not long ago that I have been a seeker all my life and am probably destined to remain a seeker for the rest of it, as for me it is not the attainment of mastery but being in the presence of mastery which gives me the greatest fulfilment, albeit vicarious. In living out my seeker's life I consider myself very fortunate indeed to have had the opportunity to travel extensively and to have seen many different practices performed as part of spiritual endeavours; however something about the fierce devotion to his circling art and the intense energy with which the Adept both explained and performed the various practices which he shared with me, have left a deep and lasting impression.

What follows is my personal account, which illustrates some of those occasions at which I was privileged to be present when, as the Adept might have put it, "I was out of the picture and there was only Tao".

I have taken the liberty of changing some names and been vague about the exact date and location where certain events occurred, however this remains a factual account given to the best of my ability to recreate what were, for me certainly, some moments of true inspiration and wonder.

A brief note on pronunciation and language.

Various Chinese names appear rendered in English letters throughout this text, most significantly that of the Adept himself. When reading names in particular, I like to be able to hear the sound in my head, as it gives me a greater feeling of connection to the person I am reading about, so in an attempt to help the reader deepen their connection to Shun Yuan, here is a note on how to pronounce the words.

SHUN is pronounced something like "SWOON" only not with a long "OO" such as in "FOOL" but with a short "OO" such as in "COOK".

YUAN is pronounced "YUEN" – imagine saying "YOU-WHEN" so that the two words blend together as one.

English is used throughout this book, however many of the dialogs which take place were originally spoken in a mixture of languages and dialects, most frequently Mandarin Chinese and English. I have done my best here to represent the tone and the feeling of the discussions and have not worried overly about creating a strictly precise reproduction. My desire is to share my story in a way which I hope is enjoyable and meaningful to others, not to attempt to act as a historian.

Chinese characters are used in two places in the text where they are a critical aspect of my experience and are accompanied by explanation or translation.

I jammed on the brakes as hard as I could, causing my scooter to swerve violently as the wheels locked up, almost throwing me off. I let it fall right there at the side of the road without thought, without any capability of thought. My mind was reeling with panic and I was sick to my stomach and desperately trying not to vomit as I leapt over the falling scooter and ran as hard as I could across the intersection to where my friend and Master lay unmoving, his own scooter a shattered wreck tangled still in the cable that had brought it down.

Chapter one.

Mrs Lim's tea house, a sanctuary in the rain.

"Lobbu!" came a voice calling from behind the counter. Disturbingly enough I looked up immediately, having become so used to Mrs Lim's mangling of my name by now that I was beginning to wonder if I would react when I got back to a world where people called me Robert. Who knows where I'd drifted off to for the last half hour?

Oh yes, the rain. The interminable pounding rain that had battered Taipei continuously it seemed since the moment I had arrived. I had been warned about the weather of course but this was getting ridiculous. It felt like it had been going on for months already. How could it still be hammering down like this?

I was half asleep a lot of the time because the roof of the apartment where I was staying was made of sheet metal and the rain crashed into it with a noise that sounded like repeating gunfire or continuous thunderclaps.

Apartment, hah! That's a good one! That was what they called the sardine can that I was going to be calling home for the duration of my stay. I was still building up the courage to complain about my lodgings when I returned one evening to find the door to the next apartment open and discovered that it was being shared by four Taiwanese students.

I decided to count my blessings, meagre as I considered them to be. I thought to myself, "at least I'm not living entirely on instant noodles like these guys"; then one night the students invited me in for dinner and I was immediately hooked. The next morning when I passed the store it took a conscious effort to not go in and buy a whole suitcase full of the delicious little packages of twisty noodles with their magical sachets of powdered chemical yummy goodness. Whatever substance the manufacturing company put in those things just had to be illegal; it was so addictive.

All my good shoes were ruined. They were well made, but obviously no match for the angry rain gods of Taiwan. The laces were all falling apart and the soles were coming away from the uppers. I was becoming gradually resigned to squelching with every step I took and as I sat wringing out my socks each evening, I wondered if I could cope if this were to be it from now on, the rest of my life lived soggy and miserable. Then I started worrying whether I had always been such a mopey git. Perhaps that was the reason I was such a loner at school. Perhaps I've got SAD, that's a real thing isn't it?

It was in the depths of one of these self-inflicted periods of moping despondency that I made the most wonderful accidental discovery. Trudging up the Lin Shen North Road looking for the address of the chap I was supposed to be interviewing that morning, I took a wrong turn. Then as a particularly fierce downpour caused the world beyond my outstretched arm to vanish before my eyes, engulfing it in an impenetrable grey mist, I stepped backwards to shelter under the extending eaves of an old house.

Most of the buildings I had seen were nondescript cubes of grey concrete, but this looked like it was a traditional old Chinese house. Being set slightly back from the alleyway gave rise to the covered porch area which was now my refuge. Having no training in architecture I was unable to tell if this were really an old building which had somehow survived despite the manic drive to redevelop that was evident everywhere, or a clever façade applied to a new building, but after a moment of standing and looking at the place I caught sight of a collection of beautiful teapots in the window, realized that it was a tea house and decided to step in. I never did get that interview done.

Opening the door caused it to set a cluster of tiny hanging bells ringing and as it closed, the noisy slashing violence of the rain outside was almost completely silenced. Inside it was invitingly warm and dry and the air hung with the blended smells of incense and tea and Chinese food cooking. Apart from a paved pathway tracing a sinuous curve across the room, the floor was completely covered in tatami, Japanese straw mats which I saw used in many Taiwanese homes.

Just as I was wondering what to do about the state of my shoes and socks, a young girl appeared and with a gesture directed me to place my shoes in a rack which stood off to one side. I call her young, going only by the clues of her bob haircut and uniform, which marked her as a senior high school student I thought; I had no ability whatsoever to distinguish the age of most of the people I met by looking at their features. She had a round face the shape of which was accentuated by the way the bob hung; her bright eyes were a perfect almond shape and she had a tiny smiling mouth. As I stood there, wobbling on one leg and peeling off my sodden socks with my fingertips, she moved off behind a wooden counter and was back a moment later with a towel in her hand.

"You should really get yourself some slippers," she announced in perfect English, with an accent that I couldn't quite place. My Chinese was coming on ok, but her fluency had rendered me entirely unable to do anything but continue the conversation in English. I wasn't immediately sure what she meant by slippers, my mind going off to the warm fluffy things that my granddad used to wear around the house, until I caught her pointing at a pair of plastic looking flip-flops.

"Oh we call those flip-flops where I come from. Where did you learn to speak English so well? Honestly if I was talking to you on the phone I'd be hard put to place you. You almost sound as if you have a regional accent but I can't quite put my finger on it."

She introduced herself as Sofia and explained that she studied at an international school and that her English teacher was from Dublin. That explained the hint of the brogue which became instantly recognizable.

Sofia led me through the tea house to a little booth, where cushions were strewn about on the tatamis and a low table sat in the middle of the floor. The walls of the booths were at my shoulder height when standing, so sitting down on the cushioned floor created a very private feeling.

"If you'd like to eat, the kitchen is open. All the food is vegetarian, oh and no MSG!" She proclaimed the last as if it were of the utmost importance and by my beaming smile in response she could tell I agreed with her.

The best restaurants I knew all around town stood out because they didn't flood the food with monosodium glutamate, the single most abused ingredient in Taiwanese cuisine; easily as bad as my Scottish grandparents' deadly abuse of salt in their cooking.

"Do you know what tea you prefer, or would you like some help choosing?" I said I'd like some help and Sofia spent some time introducing me to the various varieties of tea available and relaxing me into my newfound oasis, as I relaxed myself into the pile of cushions and started salivating at the thought of food to come.

As I waited after ordering my food and choice of tea, I sat and soaked up my surroundings. Whispers of conversation in Chinese and English floated in from other booths, mingling in the air with the constant yet barely audible refrain of what sounded like a religious chant being played on the CD player and the occasional interruption of the cluster of bells hanging inside the door. Jingling to announce each arrival and departure they made my mind wander back to childhood and to watching "Peter Pan" being performed onstage, where the part of Tinkerbelle was played by a spot of light and her voice was a similarly soft tinkling, translated for us children by Peter.

The brief wait was more than worth it, perfectly cooked Chinese dumplings "shui-jiao" swimming in a bowl of steaming broth appeared before me. I sat and inhaled the heady aromas of the soup and a grin of satisfaction came to my face as I lifted one of the plump dumplings up with my chopsticks. With dry feet and nerve endings throughout my body tingling at the pleasure-fest which was about to ensue; I had completely forgiven the angry rain gods of Taiwan for forcing me to miss my interview and offered thanks for having stumbled upon this sanctuary.

After I had finished eating, Sofia came back and introduced her mother, the proprietress whom I was to address as "Lim Tai Tai" (meaning Mrs Lim). Mrs Lim was Taiwanese through and through and spoke Chinese with such a thick Taiwanese accent that my fledgling Mandarin skills had no hope of understanding her and we were soon reduced to sign language. Sofia clearly took after her mother, although where Sofia's face seemed to be simply a place for her smile to be, Mrs Lim's face carried very complex expressions which made me think she had lived a difficult life. Through Sofia we exchanged pleasantries and after explaining that I was in Taiwan to learn Chinese and work as a researcher, I let slip that I was also very interested in learning about Chinese philosophy, particularly Buddhism and Taoism and how these were expressed in everyday life. A curious look passed over Mrs Lim's face at that moment and I wasn't sure if I had said something wrong, until Sofia said that her mother liked me and that I should be sure to come back often.

I did go back to Mrs Lim's tea house very often. The food was great, the range of Chinese teas on offer was amazing and it was cheap. Mrs Lim's tea house became my home from home and I felt like I was becoming one of the fixtures and fittings. I took to doing all my paperwork there and as much of my research as possible, hauling heavy bags full of Chinese texts borrowed from the library, along with the occasional English book when I allowed myself the luxury of non-research related reading time. I began to recognize others who visited regularly and soon found that I had a social life, which revolved around the appreciation of Chinese tea, occasional games of chess and long conversations about various aspects of Chinese culture. I became Sofia's informal English language tutor and she in turn kept introducing me to folk who spoke little or no English and thus helped my Mandarin along enormously.

It was at this time, just as I was starting to settle in and feel comfortable in my surroundings that a familiar, yet long unheard inner voice began to surface. The seeker in me was waking up hungry. Perhaps it was all the conversations with so many folks about the Chinese myths and legends in the literature I was studying, perhaps it was simply the lightening of my mood in general which had happened as the really severe period of rain had finally eased off, but something in me had stirred again for the first time in a long time and I knew it would not rest until I had satisfied it.

I started making it clear during conversations that I was interested in doing more than mere book learning and would really like to experience some of the things I was reading about at first hand. Of particular interest to me were the

Chinese martial arts and specifically those known as the internal family, whose roots were suggested by some to be steeped in Taoist mysticism and appeared on the surface to be the most accessible; after all people did Taiji everywhere, every day.

In fact I made remarkably little headway. I had really expected that one of the tea house regulars would be able to introduce me to a teacher, with whom I would at least be able to begin learning something, but time after time for whatever reason my conversation and chess buddies simply were not in a position to help me. I couldn't tell if it was something in my approach, some faux pas that I was unconsciously committing. I thought about just randomly wandering down to the park and hanging around until someone took pity and talked to me, but that didn't seem to be the right way to approach things and I began to get frustrated with myself.

Then one evening I had the dream. Perhaps it was more of a daydream. I would call it a vision but that seems to be going a step too far, even for me. In my daydream I was at Baguashan (Bagua Mountain) and had found what I was looking for. Bagua, as well as being the name of this particular mountain and the mystical symbols found in the Taoist classic the I-Ching, was also the name of a martial art, possibly the most mysterious of the internal family of arts by which I had become so intrigued. It was settled; I had to go to Baguashan.

Chapter two.

Bagua Mountain, mostly wet.

Once the decision was made to go to Baguashan I had to work out how I was going to get there. The mountain is somewhere near Taichung city which is situated a few hours' drive to the South of Taipei. I got it in my mind to get a bunch of the tea house regulars to go down with me and make a daytrip out of it and began working on a flier to put up on Mrs Lim's corkboard.

I planned a date a few weeks out. The weather had been steadily improving and I was hopeful that this would continue and provide for a really nice day out and about. I was also reliably informed that the Taichung area had the best weather in Taiwan. My spirits were high and confidence lifted further when all of the little tear-off pieces of my flier with my phone number on were gone in just a few days.

Six of the other tea house regulars, along with me, Mrs Lim and Sofia and a German gentleman called Viktor agreed to meet early one Saturday morning to have breakfast together and travel down to Baguashan for the day. I had never met Viktor before, but he had kindly offered to drive the group down in his mini-bus. He was very tall and thin with a bushy grey beard and wore his greying hair in a long pony-tail. I learned later that he had been a close friend of Mrs Lim's husband, who had passed away suddenly some years before.

I hadn't revealed to anyone that my wish to go to the mountain had come from a vision and from a desire to answer the nagging, vaguely formed philosophical questions which were coming up in my mind, but had simply said it seemed like an interesting site to visit, housing as it did an impressively large hollow Buddha with three floors inside it and behind that, the only triple-dedicated temple I had heard of, having three floors which were Confucian, Taoist and Buddhist.

That Saturday I woke up really early, full of energy and excitement. I arrived outside Mrs Lim's way too soon and resigned to the wait, I perched on the edge of a windowsill to read the book I had brought with me. This was a second hand copy of the "The Journey West", which describes the adventures of the Monkey King and his travels with the priest Hsuan Tsang from China to India.

Particularly interesting to me as a linguist was the fact that the text was presented in English and Chinese on opposite pages and that a previous owner had made copious notes, also in English and Chinese on every bit of blank space he could find. I was deeply engrossed in trying to decipher a bit of the handwritten notes when I noticed, really felt more than saw, Mrs Lim coming round the corner of the alley and approaching the shop.
"Lim Tai Tai!" I called out, but she appeared not to hear me and disappeared around a corner. Hoping for the chance of a comfy cushion to sit on, rather than a windowsill which was making my ass go numb, I jogged around the corner after her meaning to call out to her again, only there was no sign of her in the alley. At that moment I heard the front doorbells jingling and when I went around, there was Mrs Lim standing in the doorway beckoning me in. I thought to myself, "Damn that lady can move quickly when she wants to."

Mrs Lim sat me down at the table with her and offered me a huge bowl of hot sweet "do-jiang". For any prior visitors to

Taiwan, this supreme breakfast dish is already well known. To the rest of the world, to translate do-jiang as soy-milk is doing it a terrible disservice, as it bears no resemblance to the horrid soy milk usually available in high street supermarkets.

Taiwanese do-jiang comes hot or cold, sweet or salty. It is also considerably thicker than soy-milk I've had elsewhere, which tastes thin and watery in comparison to the rich creaminess of do-jiang. My preference was for the hot, sweet variety, which I swore must be the dish that inspired Chinese authors of ancient times to describe the foods eaten by the immortals in heaven.

Accompanying my bowl of do-jiang was a perfectly made "yo-tiao"; a long fried stick which you would dip in the do-jiang. As other dishes arrived on the table, Sofia sat herself down exclaiming, "You are very early". Sofia was clearly not an early morning girl and in her automaton-like state I couldn't tell if her tone was a query, a comment or a complaint at my being there and I replied simply, "Couldn't sleep."

We sat and enjoyed the wonderful breakfast and as the cloud of sleep drunkenness visibly left Sofia, I ventured a query as to where Mrs Lim had been out and about so early. "Oh mother visits with my grandfather every morning to do exercises," she replied.

"Old people in Taiwan like to get out very early because they think the energy is better" this said with a fractional shrug of her shoulders and a look on her face that appeared to be universal among the young when talking about the habits of older folks and could only mean "silly old dodderers!"

I hesitated for a minute. I had not really discussed the subject of my interest in Taiji or other things of this nature with Sofia or her mother, since that first meeting when Mrs

Lim had cast such a strange look at me upon the mention of my desire to learn about the practical, daily aspects of Chinese philosophy. To be honest I had even wondered whether the difficulties I had had in getting an introduction to a Taiji teacher may have been orchestrated by Mrs Lim because I had upset her in some way.

I decided that that was simply my own negativity and paranoia talking and that now was the moment to broach the subject. I was opening my mouth to ask a question when the door opened, setting off the jingling of the bells and in walked Viktor.

Wearing a huge dark brown cowboy hat, a long dark leather coat and remarkably ornate boots, he looked as if he was dressed for a gunfight. He was half dragging, half carrying an enormous picnic hamper through the door and I leapt up to help him and the moment to talk about things like Taiji was gone, replaced with a sinking sensation in my stomach which I recognized as I looked out of the window and realized that it had started raining again.

The rain kept coming, steadily getting heavier for the next half an hour at which point the tea house phone rang and one of the regulars announced that he was not going to make it. Over the following forty five minutes the rest of the group called in and we learned that the weather report that morning was for very heavy rain the whole day, including the area around Taichung.

I looked around the table and announced to my fellow early-birds, "I understand if you don't want to go today, but I really have to get down there. I don't mind going on the train." Sofia came to my immediate rescue, quickly explaining that her mother had arranged for people to come in and do work in the kitchen and some repairs in the tea house that had been put off for too long and that as long as

Viktor was still prepared to drive, we should certainly all go. She looked at Viktor with a pleading look that told me that there was more to this than my own simple needs. Luckily for us both, Viktor seemed entirely unperturbed by the rain, saying only that he had driven in far worse conditions than this.

"Although" he added, "this does mean that I've brought far too much sausage and bread. Oh well, the more for us to enjoy."

I almost opened my mouth to do the polite thing of refusing when I caught Sofia looking at me with a look that threatened to cast me to stone if I spoke. As soon as Mrs Lim was out of earshot, Sofia whispered something about how glad she was not to have to attend cram school that day. Apparently, sitting extra chemistry class was far from what Sofia considered a suitable use of her Saturday time.

When it came time to leave, I quietly thanked Viktor again and helped him load the picnic hamper, which he had now packed with bottles of water and cheese from Mrs Lim's cool cabinet to go with his bread and sausage. Mrs Lim had also packed various vegetarian items for herself and Sofia.

Once the hamper was stowed safely back in the mini-bus we all climbed in. I hadn't expected such luxury. The soft leather seats were the comfiest thing I had sat on in ages and easily competed with any sofa I could remember. More than this, the arm rest which came down to create my own little private space even housed a mini cd player!

Viktor did not do things in half measures I thought to myself. I settled into my seat and took out my copy of The Journey West intending to carry on reading it as we drove, but for some reason I just couldn't concentrate.

In the front, Mrs Lim and Viktor were engaged in quiet conversation. Viktor spoke Taiwanese dialect equally as fluently as he did Mandarin. Closing my eyes and listening to him, I wondered how he had managed to purge every hint of German accent from his voice, envious of his perfect fluency.

I glanced over to my right, where Sofia had donned a pair of headphones and was bobbing up and down, clearly relishing whatever music it was she had brought along with her. I waved and got her attention and when she removed the earphones I asked what she was listening to. She passed me the headphones and I put them on, fully expecting to hear the latest in Taiwanese pop blaring at me. Instead what I got was energetic, but very soulful dance music, which certainly would not have been out of place in a Chicago warehouse club. It was definitely to my taste and as she reclaimed her headphones, Sofia promised to make me a copy of the disk.

I returned to my book again. Ten minutes later I found that I was still staring at the same page and had taken nothing in at all. That familiar feeling of general dejectedness was hovering around and threatening to descend on me again. I wriggled in my seat, took a breath, went back to the book and closed it immediately in frustration and placed it on my lap; left with the rain as my major source of sensory input. Looking out of the window the world was once again occluded by a wet wall of grey.

I listened as the rain hammered down on the roof of the car and then I realized that it was making a strikingly similar noise to that which it made when hitting the roof of my apartment. I wondered to myself if my worsening mood might be in some way connected to the noise and to take my mind off it I decided to do a little experiment. I had no CD's with me, but Mrs Lim had brought along some of her own and I borrowed one of these to listen to; a collection of Buddhist chants from various countries.

The effect was so striking I could hardly believe it. As I listened to some monks performing the "Great Compassion Dharani" I could literally feel the moroseness leaving me. Although I recognized the chant as one which I had heard Mrs Lim play frequently in the tea house, I couldn't understand the words at all and simply sat for a while soaking up the sounds and enjoying the rhythm of the chanting.

The mark of a good experiment is that it should be repeatable, so I decided to take off the headphones for a while and see what happened to my mood as I was once again exposed to the noise of the rain against the roof.

It took a good long while, during which I was sure I was on a wild goose chase, but slowly I recognized the change of mood in myself and felt the negativity settling in. Once I was sure, I put the headphones back on again and felt the immediate lifting of my spirits.

I then wondered if any sound would do to cancel out the rain noise and noticing that Sofia had moved on to another disk by this time, I reached over and picked up her dance music CD. There was a distinct difference in the mood which this music produced in me, a much livelier more energetic mood; however as there was no sign of my bad spirits returning I declared my little experiment a success. Although I had always had some vague notion about the way in which sound and particularly music might affect the psyche, I hadn't really considered that the noise of the rain could have been responsible for the mood swings I had been suffering from. There was more to this that I was going to have to explore in greater depth and I once again found myself not so angry at the angry rain gods of Taiwan.

Almost before I knew it, we had arrived at Baguashan and Viktor had pulled in to a parking area at the bottom of the mountain. Mrs Lim opened the car door and got out and the rain stopped. I mean in that instant, that very moment that she opened the door and got out, the rain which had been constantly slamming down the entire time, just stopped. The sun came out and the car park was almost immediately filled with other travellers, climbing out of their vehicles and stretching their legs.

For a moment as I sat there with my mouth open, gawping like a complete idiot, I fully expected to hear birds tweeting and then to hear music playing as if I was in a scene from a Disney cartoon. Sofia reached over and shook me by the arm and out of my reverie to hurry me along saying, "Come on let's get going!"

We strolled up the mountain together and with every step, I could hear the words "tourist trap" ringing in my mind. I didn't really know what I had expected to find here, but the almost complete commercialism of the place still came as a surprise.

To me the pinnacle of this was a middle aged gentleman who sat at the base of the giant Buddha statue, dressed only in some kind of leggings, his massive pot belly on display to the world. Around his neck he wore a placard declaring that he was an immortal and inviting visitors to take a photo with him for the bargain sum of fifty Taiwan dollars.

Still shaking my head I climbed the hollow Buddha statue and looked at the various figurines and frescoes depicting moments of the Buddha's life but found nothing of particular significance, in fact I found the displays upsetting for reasons which I couldn't fully understand but which voiced themselves in my mind simply as the word "kitsch".

I announced to the others that I wanted to spend some time in the large temple which was located some way behind the giant statue and arranged to meet them again later to eat.

I entered the temple and completely ignored the first floor, which was dedicated to Confucius. I climbed up the stairs to the second floor, which was a Taoist temple, but after only a quick glance inside I could see nothing that drew me in and continued on up to the third floor. This had rows and rows of very low benches for kneeling and at the far end, a large golden Buddha looked serenely out over the space. Dotted here and there were other visitors, kneeling quietly on the benches in contemplation.

I felt immediately drawn to the peacefulness of the place, which was only heightened I felt, by the commercialism and tourist noise of the surrounding area and knelt myself down at a free spot on one of the benches immediately in front of the Buddha. I didn't really know what I was doing there, or what I expected, but suddenly a thought came to mind, a resolution; "Right. I'm not getting up from here until I know what I'm doing here and what I'm supposed to do next."

I sat and looked at the Buddha. He had done just the same thing, so the stories went. He sat down one day and refused to move until he achieved enlightenment. I wasn't aiming quite that high and thought I should at least be able to get to some kind of insight. Buddha looked back at me, utterly serene. I shifted my posture a bit, trying to get comfortable and after a while my eyes closed and I drifted off, not to sleep, but I was definitely not in a normal state of consciousness.

I had no idea how much time had passed, but I was jolted back to myself by a voice in my left ear, whispering but as clear as anything, "It's all in the breath." I got up and stretched and looked about me, really expecting to see someone standing by me, but the hall was empty.

I wandered outside and realized that a couple of hours must have passed at least and that I should go and find the others. This did not prove to be too difficult and as I approached them I apologized for how long I had been. Viktor told me not to worry about it, that they had come to find me and seen me meditating in front of the Buddha and decided to carry on without me.

"Don't worry though, we saved you some bread and sausage!" he concluded with a smile, handing me a package wrapped in white waxy paper. I was drooling at the incredible smell as I un-wrapped it and was glad that I wasn't a strict vegetarian. I thanked him enthusiastically around a mouthful of his food, "Thanks, I'm starving. This is delicious!"

We headed back to the car park, Sofia posing for photos every few seconds while Viktor snapped away with his camera and I munched on my delicious sandwich of thick bread and German sausage.

Once again we all climbed into the mini-bus and at that moment the rain started again. This time I couldn't help it, "Now that's just weird isn't it?" I asked aloud.

"The moment we got out of this bus the rain stopped and now it's started up again, as soon as we get back in. Doesn't anyone else find that weird?"

They were all looking at me like I had two heads and without them saying a word I was left in no doubt that they thought I had read far too much into a simple break in the rain. The others were simply appreciating the fact that they'd managed to have a nice time out together after all and were sorry that more of the tea house regulars hadn't braved the earlier weather.

I shrugged and gave the impression that I had dropped the issue, while internally I was thinking that there had to be something else at play here. I looked down at my lap to find that I had subconsciously retrieved my copy of The Journey West and written "It's all in the breath" in one of the margins.

Chapter three.

Inhale, exhale. Laughter fills the air.

I spent a lot of time thinking about that trip to Baguashan. Although to my companions the sudden stop-start of the rain had meant little, I was left moved by the experience and I put it alongside a few others I had had in my life which had struck me as deeply mysterious.

I recalled the first of these incidents now. Lying in my bed as a child I had been absolutely sure I was levitating and the instant I became certain of this, I crashed back down in the bed with such a thump that I was worried I might have broken it.

Later in life I had read that this was actually quite a common occurrence and had read explanations of the various strange phenomena that one might believe one had experienced while in an altered state of consciousness such as encountered when falling asleep or waking up.

These explanations always left me feeling empty in some way, in particular the way that the absolutely convincing crash back into the bed was explained away by sudden muscular contraction throughout the body. Weirdly to me, the more I was convinced by the truth of a rational explanation for mysterious phenomena, the more this feeling of emptiness, of something missing persisted in me.

Such it was with the visit to Baguashan. I didn't care if everyone else took a brief gap in the rain as a happy coincidence and nothing more. To me it had imbued the events of the day with a deeper meaning and had, to some extent, made me feel that the trip and the learning I had gained from it was of great significance.

I decided that the very next time I visited Mrs Lim's tea house I would talk to Sofia and see if I could arrange an introduction to a Master of chi-kung, the Chinese method of controlled breathing and internal energy cultivation.

I looked back at my copy of The Journey West and to the note that I had scribbled, entirely subconsciously on the page. Then I realized something else. I had puzzled over some of the notes that the previous owner had left for a long while, having no real idea what was meant by them, but now as I looked back at them with my mind focused on chi-kung, I realized that this was exactly what was being written about. As I skimmed through the book re-reading all the notes, it became clear that their author, the prior owner of the book, had understood that The Journey West was in fact a teaching tale, written entirely in metaphor and allegory and that what it was teaching was chi-kung!

I had quite a bit of work to catch up on for which I had to make use of the library computer, so it was a couple of weeks until I was able to set aside the time to visit Mrs Lim's tea house again.

I wandered up the Lin Shen North Road, enjoying the fact that the weather was good again; sunny without being too hot for a stroll. As I walked along I rehearsed what I was going to say to Sofia in the hopes that her translation to her mother would get across the right tone. Although I had no idea why, I had made up my mind by now that my progress was going to be dependent on Mrs Lim's help.

I strode on, my mind going back over my thoughts again and again, working out what I wanted to say in both English and Mandarin so that I had the best chance of getting the importance of this over to Sofia.

I found to myself wondering if I should wait until I next saw Viktor, if perhaps this topic of conversation was something that would be better handled by someone older, but I rejected the notion. Viktor did not show up at the tea house that often and I just didn't have that much of a rapport with him, while Sofia and I had become good friends as well as language exchange buddies. I would simply have to trust that she would understand how serious I was about this matter and that she would be able to convey that to her mother.

I imagined myself going with Mrs Lim in the very early morning to meet up with Sofia's grandfather, who in my mind's eye was drawn as a bit of a caricature, complete with long silky beard and all-knowing look.

I turned into the alley and walked up to the tea house and stood there dumbfounded. It wasn't there. I don't mean it was closed. The tea house simply wasn't where it should have been! I spun around a few times looking here and there as an intense confusion descended on me. What on Earth was going on? Was I going nuts?

I walked back out to the main road and looked around. I didn't recognize the buildings around the corner where I stood. It was only when I took a close look at the number on one of the buildings that I finally realized what had happened and was satisfied that I had retained my sanity. I had wandered much further north along the road than I had ever been before. Whether the tea house was where it should be I would still have to find out, but one thing was for certain, I was not where I was supposed to be.

I turned around and headed back south, walking for a full half an hour before I finally reached the correct turning and found the tea house, of course, sitting in its regular spot.

As I went in I was greeted by a girl I had not seen before who asked me to remove my shoes and showed me where to put them, before guiding me to a booth.

She had striking features, her face all angles where Sofia's was round and soft. The sharpness of her cheekbones and the way her hair had been cut gave her an elfin look, but a wild and dark elf, not the kind that fluttered gently at the end of the garden but one which belonged in the darkest depths of an ancient forest.

I told her that I was a regular visitor and asked how long she had been working there and whether Sofia was in. She introduced herself in English as Morning, the name striking a distinct contrast with my first impression of her. She told me that this was her first day and that Sofia was in the back with her mother.

I ordered "Guan Yin" tea, which had become my firm favourite and asked her, if she would let Sofia know that Robert was here and wished to have a chat with her. She trundled off, returning quickly with the tea leaves, pot and hot water and let me know that Sofia would be with me shortly. After assuring her that I didn't need any help preparing my tea, she left me to my own devices and I set about brewing my tea and reading the latest book to have caught my attention, "Jonathon Livingston Seagull" a story of the discovery of the mystical told through the eyes of a bird.

I was into my second or third pot of tea and well into my second read through of the short book when Sofia popped into the booth and sat herself down. Putting the book away I told her that I had something very serious that I needed her help with and proceeded to explain that I really wanted to learn about chi-kung and thought that perhaps her mother would be able to help me, for instance by introducing me to her grandfather.

Sofia agreed and called her mother over and repeated my request and after some exchange which went back and forth between her and her mother she looked at me and said, "It seems like you have been thinking about this for a long time Robert, why didn't you ask before?"

I told her that I had been worried that I had upset her mother when we had first met, that perhaps something in the way I had mentioned my interest was overly casual, that maybe she was worried about my interest being nothing more than an indulgence of curiosity.

As Sofia explained these things to her mother I could see her shaking her head more and more vigorously. She spoke to me directly, going slowly so that I could understand her, "Robert, you really worry way too much. Where did all of this come from? Nothing could be further from the truth. A lot of people come through here just visiting. Some of the people who stay don't even bother to learn the language, but are only here to make money. Some people really make an effort to learn about Chinese culture and language, but even among those very few have a serious desire to learn about the real aspects of Taoism and Buddhism. I will happily introduce you to someone who will be able to help you of course, but that person is not Sofia's grandfather."

After a moment's pause for thought she added, "I will take you to meet someone at a temple not far from Taipei. When would you like to go?"

We agreed to go together the following evening. I was a bit hesitant as Sofia would not be able to come with us, but decided that we would just have to make do. Mrs Lim drove us in her car, which was the polar opposite of Viktor's mini-bus. It was tiny, with no air-conditioning and appeared to have no suspension.

I had thought that chatting as we went might prove difficult, but it was actually rendered impossible as each time we went over a bump, the jangling in our bones was echoed by a worrying rattling sound coming from somewhere under the car and a loud grunt from me.

Fortunately Mrs Lim seemed to be happy just to drive in silence as there were a lot of bumps, mostly due to large potholes along the road which we took out of Taipei and into the hills surrounding the city. I was soon well and truly lost as we went along small unlit roads, then through some gates and along what appeared to be little more than a well-worn track.

It was quite dark when we finally arrived at our destination, a small compound of buildings newly-built, but quite obviously made to resemble buildings of an older period. We walked up to the larger of the buildings and Mrs Lim indicated to me that I should sit on a long cushioned bench in what I took to be a waiting room.

The surroundings were practical, not austere as such but certainly lacking the gaudiness that I had seen in other temple buildings. To the left and right of me the bench I was sitting on was almost full, yet the room was absolutely quiet. I bit down the desire to start asking all about the place and looked about me some more. Directly behind me and at head height while seated was a slot shaped window, running the length of the waiting room. Through it I could see into a very large hall, with a massive golden Buddha at the far end.

While I was looking around, I noticed a monk exit from a side room and saw Mrs Lim speaking to him and pointing towards me. The monk disappeared back into the room, reappearing a moment later and saying something to Mrs Lim with an accompanying nod. Mrs Lim crossed the large hall and popped her head around the door into the waiting room, gesturing to me to go towards the monk who was standing beside the doorway to the side room. I saw a heap of shoes at the side of the waiting room door and hurriedly shook off my shoes, before walking across the large hall to the doorway, the eyes of the large Buddha statue appearing to follow me as I went.

The monk, dressed in grey and white robes, nodded to me and gave me a warm smile as he indicated that I should follow him into the room.

As he entered, he dropped to the floor on his knees and bowed in deference to another monk, who sat behind a low table. I felt really awkward, having no idea what was expected of me in this situation and managed a half bow of my own. It turned out that "someone at a temple" happened to be the Abbot, who gestured for me to sit down at the table opposite him. As I sat down, the younger monk moved to kneel by the door.

The Abbot was a large man. To me his belly and the massive smile in his chubby round face made him look exactly like the many fat Buddha statues I had seen. "Thank you so much for seeing me," I said, my Mandarin coming out shaky and full of distorted tones so I worried he would not understand me.

"I'm afraid I'm not sure what I should call you."

"Normally the title is "Fa Shi", came the reply. I recognized Fa Shi as a title given to a senior Buddhist monk.

"Well thank you again for your time Fa Shi, I'm sure you are a very busy man. In fact I feel bad for all those other people who are sitting out in the waiting room. Have I just jumped a long queue of people who are waiting for an audience with you?"

"Would you mind then if we invited some of them in to join this audience?" he asked me.

I told him I didn't mind at all and a few moments later the Abbot dismissed the young monk at the door, who returned shortly after with half a dozen other people who had been sitting in the waiting room.

Once everyone had settled, the Abbot looked at me and asked me what it was that he could do for me.

"What is the meaning of life, the universe and everything?" I asked, probably doing horrendous injustice to Douglas Adams with my Mandarin interpretation. A strange look came over the Abbot's face and a moment later his body started to jiggle slightly, then it became clear as the smile on his face stretched into an ear to ear grin that he was trying to hold in a chuckle, which burst out a moment later as he said, "I really should answer forty two, I really should" and laughed out loud.

"It is from Douglas Adams, your question? So perhaps the answer should be too!" The words were coming out in little gasps between laughs which steadily increased in force and volume, until the Abbot was holding his sides and tears were running down his face.

His laughter was infectious. I was grinning broadly and this became full laughter as I realized that everyone else was laughing too. Then all of a sudden, the Abbot leaned across the table and grabbed me by the shoulders, his nose only inches from mine, shook me roughly and whispered in perfect English; "It's all in the breath."

I sat there instantly shocked into silence and stillness and gradually the sound of laughter around me faded away until the room was absolutely quiet again.

The Abbot had picked up some kind of carved ceremonial stick and placed this across his lap. He folded his hands into a complicated shape which I thought must be a mudra and looked out at the group sitting in front of him.

"Breath is life" he began.

"By controlling our breathing, we are able to control our being. Laughter is an excellent example. When we laugh, when we really allow ourselves to laugh aloud with no thought of embarrassment or control, we immediately have a positive effect on our being and on those around us. Laughter relieves us from stress and other sickness. In fact I have read that it may play a significant part in the battle against cancer."

The Abbot looked directly at me then and gave me the following instructions:
"Begin by breathing to a certain rhythm, breathing in for four or five heartbeats, pausing for a moment, and then breathing out for the same amount"; the Abbot demonstrated as he spoke, his fingers tracing a line in the air towards his nose and back away from it.
"Over time, gradually extend the length of your breath until you are breathing in and out only once or twice a minute. You must remain very relaxed to do this, both physically and mentally. Then focus on the feeling of the breath entering your nose and try to make it so soft that you cannot even feel it when you inhale and exhale. That is all."

The Abbot gestured to the monk kneeling by the door and the group of which I was now a part were led out of the audience room and back into the main hall, where many of them chose to remain kneeling in front of the large Buddha statue.

My head spinning, I walked back to the waiting room where I could see Mrs Lim sitting. I grabbed my shoes and walked out to the car and sat in silence as we drove back. I didn't feel a single bump and Mrs Lim had a huge smile on her face the whole way.

It was very late by the time we got back to the tea house and Mrs Lim refused to allow me to make my way home, instead showing me to a spare room above the place and inviting me to stay there the night.

I sat there in my room almost the whole night, going over and over the series of events from my dream, to the trip to Baguashan, to the meeting with the Abbot. My internal seeker was wide awake and appeared to approve. "This is it" I said to myself. "It's happening. This is what you've been looking for. Now get on with it."

I grabbed my notebook from my bag and wrote everything down for fear that I would fall asleep and lose some important aspect. There was no danger of that. The Abbot had done something to me. His sudden grabbing and shaking me while I was still laughing in an echo of his laughter had shocked me, but more than that it had really woken me up. I felt awake and alive in a way that was entirely new to me.

It was well into the early hours of the morning before I finally fell asleep and then only needed to sleep for a couple of hours before waking up again and feeling refreshed and energized.

When I awoke I could hear movement coming from downstairs and when I went into the tea house I was greeted by Sofia, not with a good morning but rather,
"My mother would like to know if you would like to have the room upstairs. She thinks you might like it better than that kettle you live in." I smiled and laughed and said thank you over and over until Sofia must have thought I was soft in the head.
"I'll move my stuff as soon as you think that's ok" I said, which turned out to be that very day.

Mrs Lim and I worked out an agreement. I took on a formal responsibility for tutoring Sofia further with her English, which I thought would be very easy; and mathematics which she had let me know she hated and which subsequently filled me with a certain dread. My maths was strong, but I hadn't ever taught anyone and now my first student was an unwilling one. In return I got the room above the tea house rent free and tea and food thrown in at staff rates, which meant practically nothing at all.

Having helped me to escape my hellish apartment, assisted me in actualizing my dream of going to Baguashan and introducing me to her Buddhist Master, the general feeling of gratitude that I felt towards Mrs Lim was growing, blossoming if you like into a much subtler yet much more powerful feeling of connectedness to her and her family, so in addition to my official duties I took every opportunity to advertise Mrs Lim's tea house among the expatriate community and over the coming weeks it felt great to see a significant increase in the number of people coming in for tea and food.

It got to the point that Mrs Lim was able to hire on two more members of staff. In addition to Morning, the first of the new girls I had met, we now had "Little Rabbit" and "Swift". All these girls insisted on speaking to me in English all the time and these were direct English translations of their Chinese names, which they demanded I use.

It was difficult enough using Morning and Little Rabbit as names and I must admit that I had to change Swift's name from the original "Swallow" with an excuse to her that it was a better translation for the Chinese "yen zi". I just couldn't look a girl in the face and say swallow without the most pornographic images coming to mind, followed by a ridiculous contortion of my face as I attempted to suppress the attendant idiot grin.

Chapter four.

A vision in blue?

I began working in earnest on the controlled breathing instructions given to me by the Abbot. My day was divided into study time, work and related research time, teaching Sofia and the associated time I needed to prepare for that, breathing work, eating and sleeping and pretty much nothing else at all.

I practised my breathing work first thing in the morning, as soon as I had woken up, taking my queue from Mrs Lim and all those other old folks and their beliefs that Sofia was so bemused by.

"After all" I thought to myself, "a billion old dodderers can't be wrong."

To start with I made a huge mess of things. I decided that I would do breaths which were six heartbeats in and six heartbeats out. The problem was I kept losing track of how many heartbeats had gone by.

I found very quickly that the mere fact of controlling my breath changed the rhythm with which my heart beat. I hadn't really paid much attention to the rhythms of my heart at all and was surprised to find my pulse changing significantly, speeding up and slowing down at every stage of the breath.

I realized after a while that I was forcing things and decided that I should lower the bar a bit and start off with four heartbeats. This felt much more comfortable and after a short while I was able to get into a stable breathing pattern.

This of course just led to the second problem, which was

that I discovered that I was an incredible fidget. How difficult could it be to simply sit still and breathe? As it turns out, pretty damn difficult indeed!

For days on end I got sudden bouts of itching and was convinced I was being eaten alive by the mosquitos which plagued Taiwan. However when a particularly vicious itch erupted on my hand during one session and there was absolutely no sign of a bite, I decided that this must be some kind of reaction to the meditation brought about by my mind and resolved to ignore the itches.

I didn't have time to test my resolve as the itching sensations disappeared almost immediately, to be replaced by pain. I had decided on a kneeling posture for my breathing work, as I wasn't able to sit comfortably cross-legged and the lotus posture of yoga was way out of my league. As I knelt one day I felt a terrible stiffness in my lower back which built up until it became really painful and refused to budge.

I was reduced to creeping around like a bent old man until one afternoon a few days later when Mrs Lim asked me what I had done to myself. I explained how the back pain had come out of nowhere and that I wasn't sure what to do about it. Mrs Lim gave me a very approving look when I told her that I had continued to do my breathing work despite the discomfort and then scolded me for not coming to her sooner.

She asked me to show her how I was kneeling and nodded sagely, advising me to make some small adjustments to my posture.

While her hands were touching my abdomen and my lower back to show me how to kneel properly, I noticed that they were very warm indeed and from somewhere recalled an article I had read about people who use a form of healing called Reiki. I asked her if she was a Reiki healer, to which she replied that she did not know what that was, but that she was indeed trying to help me with the pain in my back. After a few minutes she also produced a package, wrapped in yellow paper. This contained a number of large "plasters". These were not plasters that you would use to cover a cut or abrasion, but were medicinal plasters which had been seeped in a special tonic. I was to stick one of these plasters on my lower back each morning after showering and remove it in the evening just before bed.

The next morning I stuck the plaster on thinking, "anything has to be better than this constant nagging pain" only to swallow my words a couple of hours later. The pain was gone, but it had been replaced by a heat so intense I was seriously worried that I was going to burn all the skin off my back.

I nipped downstairs to ask Mrs Lim if this was normal and she nodded and commented on the transformation in my posture and movement from the day before. She told me very seriously that I was to use the complete package full of plasters or that I would not gain the proper benefit from them. Realizing I had no choice I gritted my teeth and did my best to put up with the burning, the severity of which died down significantly over the coming couple of days.

On the last day after I had finished off the package and removed the plaster for the evening I noticed something totally unexpected. I was having my second daily shower just before turning in for the night and saw that the drain had become clogged up and the water level was rising fast in the shower pan and threatening to flood the bathroom. Without really thinking about it I bent forward and reached down to the drain to pull away what turned out to be a plastic bottle cap.

It was at this moment that I realized how much more flexible my lower back had become. I got out of the shower and stood in the bathroom and touched my toes. I had always been able to do this, but I could now do it without any effort at all. I placed my palms flat on the floor! This was certainly new territory. I bent my body entirely in half, touching my head to my knees and stood up with a big smile, delighted with my newfound flexibility.

I went back to my room and knelt down to begin a session of breathing practice. This time I had a strong feeling that I should extend my breath further and in the end I spent the next couple of hours working on lengthening my breath until I was inhaling and exhaling to a count of ten heartbeats.

At that point I noticed that my heart had slowed right down and that I was kneeling very still indeed. I had managed to keep count of my heartbeats, but had entirely lost any sensation of time and wasn't sure whether I had already reached the point where I should be focusing on the feeling of the breath in the nostrils.

As I sat there I felt an odd sensation, like a thick warm fluid flowing down over my head and all over my body and this sensation was profoundly pleasurable in a soporific way. I slept little that night, but very deeply and awoke feeling completely rejuvenated.

The next day a package arrived for me from overseas. I had almost forgotten about the books that I had ordered and opening up the box I felt like a little child at Christmas time. Most of the books were things I wanted for work which I hadn't been able to find in any bookshop locally, but a couple were things that I had added purely for my own reading pleasure.

Once I had finished Richard Bach's "Jonathan" I had

decided that I should read "Illusions" and this was the book that I took with me back down to the teashop for my afternoon read.

I read the book once through quite quickly, being drawn easily along by the story and the style of the writing, then started into it again, taking it more slowly and savouring the characters and their adventures and really allowing myself to be in the story with them.

It was then, while I was deeply engrossed in a scene where the characters are practicing 'cloud busting', that I sensed someone standing outside the booth where I had settled myself.

After a few moments it was clear that this presence was not simply passing by, but was standing looking at me and waiting for me to acknowledge their existence. I looked up from the book, slightly peeved at being pulled away from my enjoyment of the adventure and did a double take.

A chubby old Chinese gentleman with short white hair stood at the entry to my booth dressed in a powder blue suit and white dress shirt. He looked me right in the eye and said, in English, "What are you looking for?" to which I replied in Chinese, "I'm just reading my book." He looked at the book, looked back at me and answered in Chinese, "Well I won't disturb you then" and turned away.

I looked back at the book and immediately a feeling hit me, a voice in my head shouted "Idiot! What are you doing?"

I leapt up from my cushion and darted out of the booth and looked around the tea house. I couldn't see the gentleman anywhere and there was no missing him in that blue suit. I ran out of the front door and looked up and down the alley, but again I couldn't see him. I ran around the corner to the smaller alley which ran down the side of the tea house. He wasn't there. I ran back out and up to the end of the alley and looked up and down Lin Shen North Road. There weren't that many people around and I was sure I would be able to spot him, but no, he had disappeared.

I walked back to the tea house and sat back down in my booth seriously disappointed with myself. That was an experience I was supposed to have, I was absolutely sure of it.

I glanced down at the copy of Illusions lying on the table and felt stupid. I had been reading the book and enjoying the story, but entirely failed to really learn anything from it. I might as well have spent the time reading comics or scrawling graffiti in my journal.

I was left marked by a deep feeling that I had wasted a true learning opportunity. I felt awful at my own shallowness. I felt awful at having spoken to the man in Chinese when he had made the effort to reach out to me in English. Perhaps he had only wanted someone to share a quick chat with him and I had denied him that. I felt horribly arrogant.

Other parts of my mind were chiming in with thoughts of a more fantastic nature, which try as I might I could not completely dismiss. What if this man were some kind of enlightened being who had come to me to bring some further gift of wisdom or to guide me on a journey to far flung places where I would learn the secrets of the universe. The fact that I was already in far flung places learning the secrets of the universe did not come to mind until much later.

I thought back over the brief encounter again and again. The old man had looked so odd, so out of place in his blue suit. To be honest I thought the suit itself was odd, having never seen one quite such a pale shade of blue before. All sorts of thoughts were coming up in my mind. I had dismissed this person without reason. No, that wasn't it. I had dismissed this person because I had let my own annoyance get the better of me. There was more. I had dismissed him because I was annoyed and because he looked weird and I didn't want to have to deal with a weirdo who had imposed himself unannounced on my awareness. "There" I thought. "How dare the Buddha turn up for tea unannounced? The fact that he's brought a cake with enlightenment baked in does not excuse him."

All the rest of that day I sat thinking about that old man. Late into the night and on into the early hours of the next morning I sat in my room and pondered and tried to pull something of value from the experience.

My mind flashed back to the trip to Baguashan and showed me an image of the pot-bellied immortal who I had instantly written off in my mind as a scammer. How could I possibly know whether he were genuine or not? Who was I to be making such judgements without even having spent a moment in the company of this person? Where had such a judgemental attitude come from in the first place?

These were questions I desperately needed to answer but I had no idea how I would go about doing it. One thing I could do though, while I looked for an answer to the root of these disturbing parts of my character, was to make a conscious change in the way I looked at and treated others. I wrote myself a note in my journal, reminding myself that; "The next person you meet has something of value to share with you. Take the opportunity as a gift and make the most of the experience."

I looked at the note and shook my head, there was something missing. I picked up my pen again and added, "Actively seek out these opportunities."

That very morning I decided to put my resolution into practice and after what must have been only a couple of hours nap, I headed out in search of chances to learn.

It was still quite early and the morning air was cool and refreshing. I thought of Sofia and wondered if her old people had simply come to realize over time that the early hours of the day, when the sun was still very low, were far less oppressive.

My wandering took me down to the park, all along the way exchanging a "good morning" with those I met. I walked into the park and without anything particular in mind, wandered over to a quiet area where a number of people were practicing Taiji under the trees.

I stood and watched transfixed as one old gentleman performed his exercise. He moved very slowly, but with a power and poise that was obvious even to my untrained eye and his movements had a certain fluid quality about them, so that he looked as if he was possessed by the spirit of water and his body was being used as a musician uses an instrument to express his music.

After watching for a while I wandered on and came across a group of middle aged men engaged in their practice. This was much more vigorous and the men practised in pairs as well as solo. They became very energetic indeed when they began working on a certain paired exercise and I watched intently as they tested each other, pushing to and fro.

One member of the group approached me and after enquiring whether I spoke Chinese, introduced himself as Peng and asked me if I would like to have a go. He was a short man, his cropped hair only reaching just above the level of my chin and despite his smile and the warmth of his invitation I was instantly reluctant and had to really forcefully remind myself of my resolution before I was able to step across the boundary into their practice area.

Peng explained that the exercise being performed was called "tui-shou", which means "pushing hands". I asked him if these were fighting techniques that his group were doing and he explained that the exercise should be thought of more as a way of testing one's understanding and ability to express certain principles.

He picked up a stick from the floor and using it, drew a circle in the dusty earth around his feet. He then invited me to remove him from the circle.

I looked at him with an "Are you sure?" look on my face that he clearly understood, because he smiled back and gestured enthusiastically for me to begin.

Now I'm not a small person and as I've said, Peng was. In addition to which I thought he was probably at least twenty years older than me, so I decided I had better take it a bit easy. I didn't want to end up injuring the first of my new learning encounters!

I really was that naïve. It should have been obvious what was going to happen, but as I gingerly reached out and pushed at Peng, he grabbed me and flung me almost out of the practice area!
"So" I thought "there's more to this chap than meets the eye." When I went back the second time I went all in.

I dusted myself off with my hands as I picked myself up off the floor and tried to understand what had just happened. I was bigger, I was younger, I had to be stronger, yet this man had thrown me aside like a child flings a rag doll.

I was so happy I had stopped to watch and then been able to join in! This was something I simply had to learn more about. I spent the next hour or so getting tossed here and there, my occasional tumbles to the ground eliciting profuse apologies from my partner. I loved every minute of it and when it was time to stop, I asked if I could come and join the group again.

Peng nodded and told me that the group met here most mornings from about five AM and stayed on until about noon at the weekends, when the members did not have to go on to work. He explained that his group was an eclectic one, made up of students of various teachers who had all come together to practise and share their different methods and that they had been practicing together for about ten years. I should expect he explained, to have a very different experience as I practised with different partners. I couldn't wait!

I returned to my room later that evening feeling much happier with myself. I had made a resolution and stuck to it and that had allowed me to make a connection with some new friends, from whom I was going to be able to learn something that fascinated me.

I dug out every book I had concerning the martial arts and skimmed through them, looking for information about tui-shou and trying to get an idea in my mind of exactly what it was that I was setting out to learn.

Tui-shou appeared for the most part to be an auxiliary exercise taught alongside Taiji, to help students to understand and put into practice the theories of that art. I wondered if I should be getting involved in tui-shou at all, not having had any experience with Taiji, but then put the issue out of my mind. If my new friends did not consider it a problem then I would not make a problem of it.

I thought back to my introductory session that morning, still puzzled as to how my partner Peng had managed to best me so easily. I had ended up out of breath and more than a little shabby looking; covered in dust and sweating. Peng had seemed perfectly relaxed throughout. He certainly hadn't broken a sweat and didn't even appear to have been breathing hard. I wondered how old he was and whether it would be rude for me to ask. I decided that it was important that I should know, but when I did ask him one day I was bowled over when he told me that he was in his sixties!

In my mind sixty was old, properly old. Peng's strength, vitality and agility were all at odds with my beliefs about what a sixty year old person should be capable of.

I found myself wondering where this notion had come from and this time I had a definite answer. I had spent some time in my early teens working in a care home for the over-sixties, where most of the residents had severe mobility problems and I had somehow got the impression that all people of that age must be equally incapacitated. Once again I was being shown that I needed to adjust my thinking, to accept that the notions I had developed through prior experience were not necessarily going to be useful as I went through new experiences.

Even as this thought came to mind I found myself resisting it. Something in me did not like this. It did not want to let go of knowledge which it believed to be true, even in the face of evidence to the contrary. Why couldn't I drop a stupid belief such as "All people over sixty are frail"?

I struggled with this for some time, until I caught myself thinking "All people over sixty are frail except Peng" and realized that by creating this exception, I was in fact still trying to find a way to preserve the original belief rather than to have to drop it as useless.

I wasn't sure how many other things I believed in which were equally both untrue and no longer of any use to me in my day to day life, or even causing me problems in my life by my persistently hanging on to them. This demanded further thought.

Chapter five.

A character in black, enchanted by white.

I had had to make some changes to my schedule. Starting at five in the morning meant that I needed to move my breathing sessions until just before bed. I hadn't been given any specific instructions by the Abbot as to when I should do the exercises, so I didn't think anything of making the change.

My new early morning sessions with Peng and his group became an enjoyable start to my routine, which was followed by rushing back to the tea house to shower again and get ready for the rest of the day.

It was properly hot now. The rain which had once felt like it was never going to end came now only intermittently and with none of the fury that it had displayed previously. The angry rain gods had gone on vacation, leaving their cousins the angry gods of fiery heat to watch over Taiwan in their place.

Instead of a refuge against the rain, Mrs Lim's became an oasis of coolness, relied upon by more and more people, particularly expats wishing to escape the very real risk of heat stroke. Mrs Lim did a roaring trade in iced teas and dedicated one counter to serving them alone. This gave that side of the tea house a vibrant bustling atmosphere which was great to see, because it meant that Mrs Lim was doing great business, but also meant that I would not always be able to occupy my favourite booth near the front door.

"Lobbu!" the voice came calling again, more insistent this time. Whoa! What had happened there? Where the hell had I been? I was used to my mind wandering; I'd always been a bit of a daydreamer but I felt like I'd been completely out of it for ages. I felt as if I would have been trapped forever in a wandering daydream state if Mrs Lim hadn't called out again.

I looked over to where she stood behind the counter, gesticulating wildly over towards the rear end of the tea house, obviously indicating that there was something there I should be paying attention to.

I got up, feeling slightly disoriented from being snapped so quickly back to reality and wandered over to the booth that Mrs Lim appeared to be indicating, looking back at her for confirmation that I was going the right way and getting her confirming nod and broad smile in return.

I stood in the entryway to the booth, which was occupied by a shaven-headed figure dressed entirely in black. He was sitting twisted away from me so that I could only see the back of his head and was watching something I couldn't quite make out on a tiny portable TV screen.

As I stood there my mind went back to the mysterious old gentleman in the powder blue suit and I wondered how he had felt standing outside my booth waiting to be acknowledged.

Without looking or taking his eyes off the screen for an instant, the black robed figure, for robes is what he was wearing, raised one arm and one finger in a gesture that I took to mean I should wait. I felt the sensation of becoming peeved building in me again, but before I could take a calming breath the hand was lowered and the man swung around to face me, his face glowing with a deeply satisfied smile.

I was disarmed immediately, any hint of irritation dissolved as he gestured for me to sit down and join him, pouring me a cup of tea even as I did so.

"But you are not Chinese" I blurted.

"An astute observation, succinctly put" he replied. I wasn't sure why I had expected him to be Chinese. Perhaps it was the surprise at seeing a westerner in what were clearly the robes of a monk.

"Ok, I walked into that one. Sorry, I'm not at all sure why I expected you would be Chinese," I offered.

"It's funny the expectations that we carry around with us" he replied, looking right into my eyes. I sat there and felt an oddly familiar sensation coming over me. I was gawping like an idiot again.

He rescued me from my inability to continue speaking by saying, "Thanks for waiting just now. I was watching the Opera House game and you walked up just at the most amazing moment. Do you play chess?"

As I gestured "a little" with my hands he carried on, "I think that is probably the most beautiful game of all time. Not only are there profound lessons about letting your opponent defeat himself, but the winning player was actually playing two opponents at once, who had teamed up against him."

From somewhere a chess board appeared and was quickly set up. Perhaps a look passed across my face because as he finished setting up the pieces he said, "Don't worry, it's only seventeen moves."

I watched as he moved the pieces and gave a running commentary. His focus was entirely on the board and my focus was entirely on this individual who had won me over with a smile.

I couldn't tell how old he was, but took a wild guess that he was in his thirties. His hands were small and in between moving the pieces they made gestures to go along with his commentary, which became increasingly animated until at last he concluded with a cry.

"Done!" he exclaimed. "What else could they have done except capture the queen? They simply didn't have a deep enough understanding of investment in loss and were entirely convinced that Morphy had made a fatal mistake. I've read that Isouard struggled to suppress a laugh or a gasp of excitement at that moment believing he had dealt the killing blow, only to realize in the very next moment that he had been defeated. Wonderful!"

He looked at me again then and thanked me for indulging him, "but you haven't come here to talk about chess. What can I do for you?"

I wasn't really sure what to say. Come to think of it, I didn't really have any idea what I was doing sitting in this stranger's booth, other than the fact that Mrs Lim had basically ordered me to do so.

"Mrs Lim," I started.

"Isn't she wonderful?" he replied. "Every time I come through here she is so kind to me. I think it's because she likes the way I recite the Great Compassion Dharani."

"Yes, she is wonderful" I replied, a slight tension creeping into my voice as I attempted to seize control of the flow of conversation again, or was that a twinge of jealousy that someone else should be getting Mrs Lim's attention?

"She even let me have a room upstairs for teaching her daughter" I said. "Anyway, she seemed to think that we should meet. Actually scratch that. I think she meant that I should come and meet you. My name is Rob."

"I am Shun Yuan" he replied. "Of course that is not my birth name. As you have commented I'm not Chinese. Shun Yuan is my name in religion. It's nice to meet you Rob."

"I am pleased to meet you too Master Shun Yuan." I wasn't

sure why I had added the title, but my new companion was shaking his head.

"It's not appropriate for you to call me Master, Rob. Master indicates that there is a particular relationship between us that likely began as a teacher-student relationship and has grown in depth over time. In the Chinese, as I am sure you know, it has connotations of a father and son relationship too. If the title is important to you, it would be better for you to refer to me as Adept Shun Yuan."

I nodded understanding and not knowing what to say next I picked up the cup of tea which he had poured for me and took a sip. It was very different to anything else I had tried, having a deep fruity aroma which reminded me of mulled wine more than anything. Shun Yuan smiled at my appreciation of his tea and told me that he had brought it from mainland China for Mrs Lim.

"So," he said. "We shouldn't risk making Lim Tai Tai cross with us. I understand that you are a student of the internal arts. I'm sure you can see the parallels with the game that I just played through."

I had to admit then that my attention had not been on the moves or his description and for a moment I was sure that he would run through the whole thing again. I was just enjoying sitting and talking and really didn't want to have to sit through a chess history lesson.

Shun Yuan just smiled and cleared away the board. "Why don't you start by telling me what it is that draws you to the internal arts" he asked, "and I'll see if I can help you in any way."

I thought this was going to take some time. I didn't really have a clearly articulated reply in my mind for myself, let alone one which I was ready to give to someone else.

I began by describing my fascination with the esoteric

and with those who worked to discover mysterious truths. I talked about the feeling of fulfilment I had gained from my meeting with the Abbot and that I continued to gain when practicing my breathing exercises.

I explained how there had been occasions throughout my life to which I ascribed a certain beauty and importance because they were mysterious and inexplicable, but how at the same time I longed for an explanation of those events that didn't leave me feeling empty.

I shared the fascination I had with Chinese language and how that had led me to a study of Chinese belief systems and how I dearly wanted to learn more about these things in a practical sense.

What I really wanted, I said, was to learn how one would live one's life in accordance with these principles which were so beautifully put in writing. Shun Yuan sat and listened, his focus never leaving my face for an instant and let me go on and on. After some time I realized that I was repeating things I had said before and stopped myself.

"My god I'm rambling. I'm sorry."

"Are you hungry?" he asked quietly. I was famished. It was getting late and I hadn't eaten for a long time.

"Let's go somewhere else to eat," he said, "I'd like to show you something."

Shun Yuan got up and went to the counter to have a brief chat with Mrs Lim, after which he gestured from the front door for me to follow him.

We left the tea house and walked down to the main road and turned to head north. As we walked I couldn't help noticing how Shun Yuan moved. In his walking I could clearly see hints of what the old man doing Taiji in the park had been expressing. There was such fluidity about his motion that he appeared to be made of liquid.

He walked quickly; enough that I had to make an effort

to keep up, despite the fact that he was a lot shorter than me. When we crossed at the junction of a small alleyway and he stepped off the kerb and then up again on the other side, it was as if he had floated across the gap. His head did not appear to bob up and down as I knew mine did, but seemed to float along always at the same level. I looked closely at his feet, wanting to make sure that he was not in fact floating along and felt foolish when I saw his foot plant firmly on the floor with each step.

I was just framing a question in my mind about his walk and whether it was part of his practice when we arrived outside a shop, the sign above proudly announcing that this was "The Brothers Li Noodle Paradise".

Shun Yuan turned to me and softly said, "Before we go in Rob, I want to let you know why I've brought you here. Just now at Mrs Lim's, when you were talking about the things you were hoping to learn, you quickly drifted away into a very abstract description. I've brought you here to begin trying to help you find the answers you are looking for, while keeping your feet firmly on the ground."

That said Shun Yuan walked in and loudly called out for one of the Li brothers, who came and greeted him as an old friend and complained at the length of time since the Adept had last visited. We were shown to a table right next to the open kitchen area where the brothers made their noodles. "You are studying chi-kung Rob," Shun Yuan said.
"If you want to know about the real meaning of gungfu, keep your eyes peeled. Don't look away and try not to blink" he concluded smiling.

The younger of the two Li brothers had picked up a huge blob of dough and rolling it briefly on the table he created a long dough-snake, about the thickness of my arm and at least twice as long. This he started to twirl and spin in his hands in various ways, so that the dough-snake continually twisted and wrapped around itself, occasionally displaying patterns such as I had seen when girls braided their hair.

It was an interesting display but I was just beginning to wonder what the point was when all of a sudden, the dough-snake transformed into perfect strands of noodles hanging from the outspread fingers of younger Li's two hands.

The metamorphosis from a single gloopy rope to dozens of beautifully formed thin noodles was so immediate and so complete that it felt watching a magic trick.

Shun Yuan looked over at me and asked, "What's the first thing that comes into your mind watching that?"
"I thought it was like magic," I replied.
Shun Yuan nodded.
"Like magic, ok" he said. "Do you know the saying that a technology far enough advanced beyond the level of an observer would appear to be magic?" I nodded in reply and he continued, "It's the same thing with skill Rob. What you are looking at is something very concrete and mundane. He's making noodles out of a blob of dough. His skill is so good however, that it appears like magic to your eye, and to mine I might add. The point I'm making here is that you needn't drift off into some vague fantasy realm to experience wonder. The things you are reading about, the Tao which has so captured your imagination is rooted in the ordinary and the real; it is all around you all the time if you only look."

I sat silently taking this in while Shun Yuan went on. "Much of the time, the work of practitioners of Tao or other ways which might be labelled esoteric or mystical, are branded as magical simply because the lay people observing those works have no other means to explain them or even discuss them. What's more, if you were to ask younger Li how he just did that, I guarantee he would not be able to tell you. He might be able to teach you the steps that he took in learning how to eventually come to his current level of skill, but to him these days, he simply wills the noodles to come out of the dough. His focused intent is paramount in achieving his goal. The mechanics of what he is doing with his body, how his arms move, how he twists his wrists, how his fingers wriggle in just such a way have all become less significant to him. Of course they are still important, but only in so far as they are a vehicle or a tool for translating his intent into physical action. It is his mind that creates form out of formlessness, noodles out of a blob and that is exactly why it feels magical to you and me."

He stopped for a moment, leaning over the table and reaching into a bowl of flour, then scattered a handful on the table top in front of us.

"I know you are a Chinese scholar, so don't take offense at what I'm about to do. I'm giving you something which I hope will help you with your development, I'm not giving you a lesson in etymology ok?"

I nodded in agreement and he proceeded to write the characters "gung" and "fu" in the flour on the table. My mind instantly raised images of Bruce Lee in "Enter the Dragon", David Carradine in the TV series "Kung Fu" and countless other images and tales which had all been woven together in creating my understanding of this term.

功

"This word," he said pointing to the character "gung". "What does this mean to you?" I gave him the regular meaning of "achievement" in reply, which he agreed with but asked if I would elaborate. I talked about the connotations of effort and skilled work, which appeared appropriate given the demonstration we had just witnessed and he was happy with this.

"So the 'gung' character" he said, "means an achievement that we have made by the application of our efforts through some skilled means." Then he pointed again and asked,

夫

"Then what is this 'fu' all about?"

I sat and looked and for the life of me I couldn't come up with anything which seemed to fit the lesson that I thought Shun Yuan was trying to get across. I resorted once again to the dictionary meaning with which I was most familiar.

"Well 'fu' means man" I said, "or perhaps mankind, so maybe the whole thing is talking about human achievement?"

Shun Yuan rubbed his hand over the flour, erasing the words he had written and wrote four other characters.

人大天夫

These were "Ren" meaning man, "Da" meaning great, "Tian" meaning heaven and lastly "Fu" also meaning man.

Written this way from left to right there appeared to be a development in complexity of the characters, with each building on the one before. I swallowed down my immediate reaction, which was that this was not what I had been taught in Chinese class and it didn't fit the way the Characters were formally written and tried to understand the point he was trying to make.

Shun Yuan confirmed this progression I had noticed to be the point he was making.

"By the application of his efforts" he said, "through some skilled means, man becomes great." As he was saying this he drew a line from the first to the second character.

"In time his greatness will come to equal the heavens," he continued, drawing a line from the second to the third character.

"Eventually, the achievements of man will transcend the very heavens themselves" he said, pointing at the last character, which I agreed did look very much like a tiny spark ascending above the character for heaven.

I had never heard such a description of the meaning of gungfu before and I took his unorthodox explanation as a further driving home of his message that the wondrous was rooted in the everyday and that one of the keys to discovering it for yourself was in being persistent.

"Human achievement indeed," continued Shun Yuan, "if we are using that term in the sense of pushing the boundaries of human achievement and really exploring human potential!"

Just then older Li came over and stood at the table next to ours, chatting with the customer who was sitting there. He held a large ball of dough in his left hand and a strangely shaped cutting implement in his right and while carrying on his conversation, without even looking at what he was doing, he made small chopping actions with the cutter which caused little "bullets" of noodle dough to fly off and land in a wok full of steaming broth. In just a few seconds he had reduced the large ball of dough to a third of its original size and did not miss the wok with a single dough bullet.

Shun Yuan looked at me and shrugged and said "What a show off!" then laughed loudly and slapped me on the back and warned me not to take things too seriously.

When we had finished our noodles, I got up quickly intending to pay, only to be informed by older Li that it was already taken care of. I turned around to thank Shun Yuan for the meal and found he was already gone.

I shrugged my shoulders and said, "It figures" to myself and left the aptly named Noodle Paradise to head home. As I walked back to the tea house I went over and over the events of the evening in my mind.

For all the effort I had put in, all the hours of studying and research trying to get to an understanding of Tao and what it meant, Shun Yuan spoke of these things in a way that made them immediately accessible to me and allowed me to become part of a flow of events that I had not previously truly experienced. He had in a way offered the beginnings of an answer which did not leave me feeling empty and I realized that that is exactly what I had asked for. I spent the rest of the walk home wondering how I would make contact with him again and hoped that if he did not show up at the tea house, Mrs Lim would have some way of getting in touch.

That evening as I knelt doing my breathing, the thick sensation of warmth once again came over my body and I became incredibly still. With my mind I tried to feel my breath coming in and out of my nose, but could not. I tried to feel my heart beating, but could not. I forgot all about my breath. My body seemed to be dissolving away and the very last sensation that I felt was the tips of my two thumbs as they gently touched one another, then it was all gone. For a time I knelt there, feeling like a disembodied awareness until a further change began happening. My awareness could feel itself, vibrating with a certain frequency. It could also feel that there was a space-time around it which also had a certain vibrational frequency and it seemed that these variations in frequency were all that distinguished the one from the other. Gradually the frequency of my mind began to change and grow closer and closer to the frequency of the space-time I was in, until I could barely distinguish one from the other.

The last thought I remember having was a moving image; a single drop of water as it made contact with the surface of a completely still lake and was absorbed, in that moment sending ripples running across the entire surface of the lake.

I have no idea how long I knelt like that, but the sensation of air coming in through my nostrils brought me back to myself and I opened my eyes and looked around my room.

I was definitely not back to a normal state yet. As I looked at my blankets their softly rumpled shapes made them appear to be breathing. On the wall opposite, a hanging which I had never taken much notice of, depicting the journey of the Eight Immortals as they crossed the sea had become animated.

I glanced down at my own hands and was surprised at how large they looked! They didn't appear swollen, but they were certainly much bigger than usual. I decided to move a finger just a fraction and found it to be an act requiring the most intense concentration.

Although I hadn't intended it, as my forefinger moved the rest of my hand moved and in a moment I found myself standing up and stretching and the world, or at the very least my perception of it, had returned to normal. My rational mind came alive with questions, as if it was feeling left out due to all the time I was devoting to answering the needs of my inner seeker. Is there any difference between the world and my perception of it? Is there a world which exists whether or not I perceive it?

I rummaged through my cupboard and pulled out a battered copy of Gary Zukav's "Dancing Wu Li Masters". This book had come highly recommended to me by one of the tea house regulars when he had given up trying to explain some aspects of particle physics to me. He had been trying to help me understand that many of the theories of quantum mechanics had a profound resonance with those found in Taoism and other oriental traditions. "Read this" he had said, continuing with a cautionary, "but beware, it's going to twist your brain."

I put the book into my backpack and a quick glance at the clock told me that it was shortly after five in the morning, so I hurriedly got the rest of my things together and went off to the park.

Chapter six.

The first method.

Pushing hands. Magnetic hands. Electric hands.

I arrived at the park to find that Peng and his friends were already well into their practice. This would certainly make things interesting as I had noticed that they began their morning sessions very gently and slowly indeed, gradually building in force and intent as they went on.

I stood quietly at the edge of the practice area, which seemed to be the thing to do until one was invited over the boundary. The boundary itself was a low ridge of earth, running in a large oval and created by half-burying and covering over a thick rope, such as might be used to tie up a ship at a mooring.

It was a nice space, with several trees standing inside the boundary and stone benches dotted around on the outside. These tended to be covered with the work clothes, briefcases and other bits and pieces belonging to the group and I felt completely at ease putting my backpack among them, despite the horror stories I had heard from others about bags being stolen.

One concession to safety which I made in this respect was to always carry my passport on my person in a specially made waist band, along with some emergency money.

As Peng gestured to me to approach, I dropped my bag on one of the benches and thought it odd that there were so few other things piled up there, as the whole group appeared to have turned out that morning.

I put that and any concerns for my own bag out of my

mind as Peng took me through some exercises which soon turned into a playful session of tui-shou, which at that moment I came to think of as "Raggedy Rob Doll Time."

I smiled to myself at this, a big smile which caught Peng's attention and caused him to stop. He turned and said something to the rest of the group in Taiwanese dialect, which attracted a round of applause from the rest of the group which appeared to be directed at me!

"I'm not sure what you said" I gasped out, my lungs taking full advantage of the break in the exercise to suck in as much oxygen as they could.

"I feel like an idiot most of the time." Peng spoke to me in English then. Really bad English, but I could tell he was being very serious and obviously thought that hearing what he had to say in my native language was important for me, so I listened hard.

"When you started practicing with us, I told you that relaxation was the most important thing; that you should take it easy and that you shouldn't worry about winning or losing. In fact you should learn by investing in loss." My ears pricked up at that phrase. Hadn't that been what Shun Yuan was talking about when he was describing the chess game?

Peng continued, "You are one of the few people who have taken immediately to that advice, to remain relaxed and fluid despite being thrown all over the place. Although I have seen this in you before, your smile just now was a big sign that you are relaxed not only physically, but mentally and emotionally." Peng took me by the arm and led me out of the practice area, giving a faint nod of the head to his group as we left.

We walked over to another area of the park where a small group were training in similar methods.

"These are Master Wu's students" he explained and

continued by pointing out one individual.

"Over there is Master Wu." Master Wu was working with one of the students, practicing tui-shou techniques which were, to my eye, very similar to those used by Peng and his group of friends. The Master was tossing the student here and there with a casual effortlessness, as it seems Masters will.

"Watch the student very closely," said Peng.

"Watch his body. Watch his face, particularly his mouth."

I watched intently and after a short while some things became apparent. First, that every time the student got pushed, or thrown or simply stumbled and fell, it was because he had overextended himself. At first glance, one might have assumed that the Master was bullying his student, deliberately pushing him around in order to boost his own ego in front of an audience, but on close observation this was absolutely not what was going on.

The movements of the Master appeared to only have the impact they did because of the way the student had unbalanced himself. Frequently these moments came when the student attempted to press home an advantage that he thought he had gained.

Something else became quite obvious too. The student was not relaxing. His body was tensing up, his lips became pursed and his breathing erratic and shallow. I turned to Peng and nodded and then thanked him for the lesson as we walked back to his practice area, where he spent time pointing out the different strengths of the members of his group.

"I don't show you any specific technique" he said.

"What I am trying to do with you is to find out which principle will work best for you to begin with, so that I can pair you with the right person to teach you that."

"Why can't I just pair with you?" I asked.

"It's been working so far hasn't it?" Peng thought for a moment and then agreed. He explained that the principle he worked with was a strong shaking force and he showed me how he generated this force with his entire body and let it travel out through his hands. I could see ripples of energy travelling up his body and along his arms as he demonstrated.

"Even in playing the piano" he went on, "the entire body must be involved, not just the hands, or the music will not be right. So imagine how much more important that is when you are doing tui-shou!"

Peng called over another member of his group and showed me how he used his shaking force to destroy the balance of his opponent. Each time he did this he followed up by throwing his opponent to the ground, something which I had not noticed him doing before.

Another member of the group came over and joined us. This was Mr Tsai. With his full head of grey hair he appeared to me to be the oldest member of the group and he moved slowly and deliberately. He was also a very quiet man; in fact I didn't think I had ever heard him speak.

He and Peng crossed hands and began performing a repeating exercise that I had seen others in the group doing, intermittently pushing and yielding. Their bodies had a gentle swaying motion back and forth as their hands went round and round in a circular pattern which reminded me of the ubiquitous Yin and Yang symbol.

Suddenly, with a ferocity that took me completely by surprise and made me gasp out loud, Peng grabbed tightly onto Mr Tsai's arms and performed his favourite shaking technique. I had been on the receiving end of that technique enough times, although never had Peng exerted anywhere close to this amount of force when practicing with me, so I just knew that Mr Tsai was going for a dust bath.

I am glad I didn't blink just then. Mr Tsai did not even wobble. He stood there, utterly motionless except for his arms, which were only moving because Peng was giving them a violent shake. His arms certainly resembled the rag doll that I became at such moments, but the rest of his body was perfectly still.

I thought he was just like a tree in a gale, the branches bending and swaying with the force of the wind but the central core remaining still and erect. Peng stepped away and the two men bowed deeply and very formally to each other, before big smiles broke out and Peng announced, "I almost had you! I was so close that time!" and I heard Mr Tsai's voice for the first time as he replied.

"That's getting much closer my friend. I think in a year or two, your shaking fist is going to surpass my relaxed fist". I couldn't help the look that came over my face. Mr Tsai's voice was a soft, but very high pitched squeak and it was no wonder I had not heard it carry across the practice area. Thankfully nobody was looking at me at that moment and I apologized to Mr Tsai internally for the instant judgement which had come to my mind, "Weird."

Peng explained that he had been working for years on his one technique and that he had bettered all the other members of his group except Mr Tsai, who had taken the ability to allow an opponent's energy to flow through him unhindered to new heights.

We began working then on specific methods for me to train. He showed me how to grab my opponent so that my fingers were not in danger of being seriously damaged. He demonstrated how I should sink my weight into my posture and develop what he called "rooting force".

It was while Peng was going through a sequence of movements with me, for what seemed like at least the tenth time that I asked "What time is it? Don't you have to start packing up for work?"

"It's Saturday Rob." The reply, so normal in any other circumstance almost floored me. I had lost a day. I had been completely convinced that this was Friday. I had missed class. I had missed meetings. I had missed Sofia's study time. I had not eaten or drank or peed or been aware of doing anything that whole time.

I ran over to the bench, with the briefest of nods to Peng as I crossed out of the practice area, tore open my bag and grabbed my wallet. I was something of an obsessive when it came to keeping receipts and ticket stubs and the like, but I had nothing for Friday. The last date on anything I had was on a receipt from a shop where I had bought a bottle of water and this had Thursday's date on it.

"Are you ok?" Peng asked. I hadn't even noticed him approach, my brain still reeling as it was from the gap in time. I replied that I was ok, but thought I'd better head back home as I was having trouble recalling the events of the previous day and was beginning to feel quite anxious about it. Peng offered to drive, which I gratefully accepted and before long I was back at Mrs Lim's tea house.

Mrs Lim wasn't around, but I found Sofia sitting in one of the booths reading an English book. As she looked up at me she said, "Oh you are out and about then. You've left the sign on your door and I wasn't sure."

"Sign?" was all I could manage in reply.

"Mum put a do not disturb sign on the door. She said she popped her head through your door on Friday to see if you were ok and found you in the middle of some intense meditation, so she left you to it and put the sign up."

I stood there, still feeling odd. My immediate fear; that I was suffering from some terrible brain disorder which was causing me to lose chunks of time was gone, replaced by complete disbelief that I had spent the entire time from

Thursday night after my meal with Shun Yuan, until the early hours of Saturday morning kneeling in meditation in my room.

I nodded and mumbled a vague apology to Sofia about missing her time on Friday and was about to turn and go when she said, "I really need help with this! I can't understand a single word of it!" This was strange coming from Sofia as her English skills were exceptional, my tutelage only really being needed on the rarest of occasions, or when Sofia wanted a written piece to have a particular flavour.

Her call for help had broken me out of my daze at least and I settled down in the booth with her and took the book. A noise came out of my mouth then, I think was trying to say "Oh" but it came out as a strangled gurgling sort of gasp.

The book in my hand was a copy of TS Elliot's "The Wasteland" and was so far out of my league that I was left once again, feeling like a complete idiot.

Such was my surprise that she had been assigned this poem that without thinking I asked Sofia if I could talk to her teacher before we began working on it. I wasn't really sure if I was doing anything but stalling for time, but Sofia seemed to think it was a good idea and said she'd arrange for a class get-together at the tea shop one evening.

I sat there for a while feeling that I'd had a psychological battering from multiple directions at once. My mind felt like Peng had taken hold of it and shaken it almost clear out of my head and I wished that I had an inkling of the understanding that Mr Tsai had demonstrated when he stood unruffled against Peng's onslaught.

As if all this mental excitement and confusion were not already enough, for some reason I reached into my backpack and took out the book I had put there. The previous owner, the tea shop regular who had gifted the copy to me had been right; it twisted my brain. When I went to my room that evening I fell immediately into a deep sleep and slept like the dead until the next morning.

Upon waking I checked the clock which showed the time at a quarter to five. I pressed the little button which would cause it to show me the day and date and was relieved to see that it was Sunday.

I went down to the park and joined in with Peng, assuring him that I felt fine and had just had a weird couple of days. Peng had me start practicing a simple version of a technique which he said had eventually developed into what everyone called his "shaking fist".

After spending the morning working on that one simple movement, I thought I was beginning to get the hang of it. Peng had me practise with several other members of the group, all newcomers themselves and I handled myself well, managing to make a couple of successful throws to the ground while not being thrown myself.

At lunchtime I left the group to continue their practice, wanting to return to the tea house to see if I could arrange to bump into Shun Yuan. If he did not show up, I had decided I would ask Mrs Lim where I could find him. I sat for a while waiting for him to show and eventually decided that he wasn't coming, so I asked Mrs Lim if she knew where I could find him and she wrote down the address for me.

It was a long way across town and after a few minutes of arguing with myself I took Sofia up on her offer to use her scooter. I had ridden motorcycles and scooters before, but was apprehensive about the traffic in and around Taipei. Various cities in the world compete for the title of world's worst traffic and claim to be home to the world's worst drivers, but in my opinion Taiwan beat them all.

I was very cautious indeed as I crawled my way across town, by far the slowest moving object on the road including I might add an old man on a bicycle who overtook me. At least I arrived in one piece and still in a fraction of the time it would have taken to walk and not drenched in sweat as I would have been if I had taken the horrendously overcrowded bus.

As I turned up the alleyway I could see Shun Yuan, sitting on a porch and drinking from a huge blue bowl. He spotted me and called out a welcome and in moments we were sitting together on the porch. I politely refused his offer of a bowl of soup and he asked how I had been.

"Did you do something to me?" I asked. I went on to explain about the missing day spent meditating.

"What kind of answer do you want?" he replied.

"I would like to give you a real answer, but given what you've been through recently I'm not sure you are in the right state to hear it." I didn't even hesitate before answering, "I really need to hear it. If I think I'm going to freak out I can always escape on the scooter!"

He laughed at that and said, "There is no you; there is no me. There is no doing. There is no something." I recalled a book I had been reading on the use of a form of questioning called "Koans" in Zen Buddhism, which were designed to provoke intense insights and immediately asked him, "Who just said that?" He replied by grabbing another bowl from where it lay on the floor, this one made of metal and having a carved wooden stick in it. He took the stick in his hand and struck the bowl, which made a metallic ringing noise like a gong. I wasn't sure if this was his answer, so I asked him to explain.

"Rob, if you are going to play 'spring the Koan without warning', you either have to make sure you are delivering a finishing blow, or you have to be ready to go one round or two!"

"Where did the ringing sound come from?" he asked. I replied that the bowl had made the ringing noise and he went on asking, "what about this wooden striker?" holding it up in his hand.

"What about my hand, my arm, my intent? What about the air around the bowl? What about your ears? All of these things are intimately involved in the experience of hearing the ringing sound you just heard. All these things, which your mind perceives as separate isolated objects are connected as one in that experience of ringing." I thought I understood what he meant.

"So, when you say that there is no you and no me and no anything else, what you really mean is that these things only appear to be distinct things" I ventured. He nodded and said, "That'll do for now. What's next?"

I had driven out here without knowing whether I'd find Shun Yuan or having any clear idea what I wanted to say to him, but I blurted out, "I go out to do tui-shou in the morning with some friends and do my chi-kung and meditation at night. I read somewhere about Yin chi and Yang chi and wondered if you could help me understand that a bit better. I certainly do feel a big difference in the quality of my own energy in the day compared to at night."

Shun Yuan sat thinking for a moment and then explained that there were many different interpretations of what he was about to tell me and that I shouldn't think of his as any more right or wrong than any other. This was simply his understanding being expressed in his own way.

I told him I understood and he said, "For me there is no Yin chi and Yang chi. Yin and Yang are the polar opposites from which apparent reality is composed, but true chi belongs to neither of these poles. In my Order we think about Yin and Yang as two great dragons swimming about in the void and chasing each other. The bodies of these two dragons continually slide one against the other and this action generates an energy, which we are now calling chi."

He had me hold my hands up and clap them hard and then vigorously rub them together. After a while he asked me to stop.
"This warm tingling sensation that you feel now, is it left tingling or right tingling?" he asked.
"Chi is just like that. It doesn't belong to one pole or the other, but arises out of the interaction of the two poles."
"If there is no something, how are there two poles?" I asked. In response Shun Yuan picked up his wooden striker again and said, "Let's remember that by 'no something' we meant there are no really separate things, meaning that all things are connected. Here look, there is only one stick, but your mind divides it into left and right. The two poles of Yin and Yang are not separated by anything but your mind, just as the left and right sides of the stick are not separated. In fact, if you try chopping the stick in half to separate left and right, you find of course that both pieces still contain the complete picture."

A question popped out before I had even realized I was going to ask it.
"I feel like I am making real progress with my chi-kung, but it's still a thing that I do separate from anything else. How can I use what I am learning while doing my chi-kung to help my tui-shou get better?"

A long pause followed while Shun Yuan appeared to be mulling over what he should tell me.
"Ok, I'll give you a method to work with which may help you" he said and asked me to hold out my two hands in

front of me as if they were holding a small ball between them. He took me through some exercises then, having me imagine the ball filling up and deflating as I breathed in and out, but after a while he shook his head and said, "No, not like that. You are too much in your head. You have to be in the ball."

With that he took my right hand and placed his two hands on either side.

"Are you going to teach me some healing hands?" I asked. "I have read something about Reiki and Mrs" I stopped abruptly. I had initially noticed strong warmth coming from Shun Yuan's hands, which is what had caused my comment, but now something else entirely was happening.

It felt like a pressure was building, getting stronger and stronger as I sat and looked at my hand and felt it getting gradually squashed. Far from being hot, Shun Yuan's hands now seemed to be emitting a cold breeze. He moved his right hand ever so slowly until the fingers were pointing at my palm and then drew a circle with those fingers just millimetres away from my skin.

I could feel a cold point on my skin and felt it move down and around as he traced the circle with his fingers. Just at the point where the circle became complete and I was completely entranced by what was going on I felt a shock, like a powerful spark of electricity which struck me in the palm and travelled up my right arm.

I leaped up out of my seat with a cry, my arm flailing about and knocking flower pots off the ledges where they had been placed. I tumbled backwards out of my chair and landed heavily on my back, winding myself in the process.

"What the hell was that?" I demanded. To which Shun Yuan said, "You tell me. You did ninety nine per cent of what just happened, flailing about like that and smashing up my hosts flower pots!" I wasn't going to be put off.

"You know exactly what I mean" I said, "what was that and how did you do it?"

"It's just not sinking in is it?" he asked.

"Perhaps it was a poor choice of example."

"Then show me another one!" I said eager for more of the same.

Shun Yuan stood then and led me off the porch to a grassy area beside the house. He stood in front of me and without any warning at all he thrust his forefinger at my belly. My body reacted, instantly doubling over; though whether in reaction to something he had done or in fear or anticipation of what might be imminent I wasn't aware and never did have any time to work out.

As I doubled up my head had struck his and as I fell to the floor I thought that this must be what it is like to head-butt a bowling ball.

"I'm sorry" he said. "That is going to bruise badly. I didn't expect your reaction to be quite so energetic and was too slow getting out of the way. Let me see if I can find something so we can prevent you having a black eye."

A few minutes later he returned with a damp cloth which had a similar smell to the medicinal plasters that Mrs Lim had given to me.

"Perhaps I'm just thick" I said as I nursed my head.

"But you are going to have to explain to me how you did that."

Shun Yuan had the oddest look on his face, which called to mind the look my physics teacher had given me after trying to explain a concept to me for the hundredth time and getting only my blank stare in return.

"I am not trying to be difficult" he said, "but you must understand this. That was not something that I did to you. In a very real sense everything that has happened is a thing done between us. It's like we are dancing a dance, with me

doing my steps and you doing your steps. It's just that in this dance just like in tui-shou, I have a different intent, which is to upset your centre and take advantage of that while you are off balance. What I failed to realize is how tightly wound up you had become, so the slightest trigger was enough to cause a massive reaction."
"Perhaps you are right" I said.
"Perhaps I'm just not ready to be able to hear what you are trying to share with me, but I have an idea. Would you agree to come to the park with me? Perhaps if you were to demonstrate your method with my friends there, we would be able to come to a better understanding."

Shun Yuan nodded in agreement and we arranged that we would meet at the park the following Sunday, when we would have the whole day to practise again. I was hopeful that a good number of Peng's group would be around as I really wanted to see what their reaction would be.

After assuring myself by prodding and poking at my face and head that I had not suffered any permanent injury, I climbed on the scooter and rode home.

Chapter seven.

The second method.

A big circle, a small circle, an empty circle.

I slept poorly and woke late the next morning, so by the time I had made it down to the park Peng had already left and the other members were packing up to get ready to go to work.

Monday morning tended to have the lowest turnout and the session was typically the shortest of the week. I mooched around the park for a while, watching other groups going through their exercises, but not feeling the desire to join in.

It was only about nine o'clock on that Monday morning when I caught myself thinking that the week was dragging. I was completely caught up in anticipation of what would happen the following Sunday.

I imagined that ancient alchemists must have felt this way when they were first experimenting with mixing various elements together; excited at the possibility of turning lead to gold, but anxious in case they blew the roof off the laboratory. I hoped that in asking Shun Yuan to come and demonstrate his methods to my friends in the park, I hadn't unwittingly put elements together which would have a violent reaction and explode, taking me and everyone else in the park along with them.

I went through the motions with my study and work. I'd been doing that for a while now anyway. I was bored with what I was studying and was getting passing grades without applying any real effort. I could have done my work in my sleep and the fact that I hardly needed to spend any money made me wish repeatedly that I could just quit altogether and focus entirely on chi-kung and tui-shou and perhaps learn more of the other internal arts.

I started working Shun Yuan's advice into my chi-kung time. I sat and did my breathing as usual and held my hands in front of my body as he had shown me, as if they were holding a little ball. I focused on visualizing the expansion and contraction of the ball as I breathed in and out, but I felt always that I was still too much "in my head" and was completely unable to get into the ball as I had been told.

Tuesday and Wednesday passed with me going about my life on autopilot, moving like a metronome tick-tock from one activity to the next. I kept finding myself recalling bits of conversation with Shun Yuan and meaning to write down questions that I wished to ask him, but somehow my usual habitual note taking wasn't happening and when the end of the day came, I got repeatedly stuck with questions on the tip of my tongue that I just couldn't get right.

Wednesday evening provided the first break in what had otherwise begun as an intolerably slow week, when a group of students from Sofia's English class turned up at the tea house for dinner one evening. Along with them had come Sofia's teacher Gerald, who I could not help thinking of as leprechaun the moment I laid eyes on him.

Gerald was tiny, balding on top with a mass of uncontrollable red hair covering the sides and back of his head. To add to this, he had chosen a bright green suede jacket to wear over his jeans that evening. I saw no hat and caught myself looking for his Shillelagh. I put Gerald in his late fifties and wondered what had brought him from an emerald isle, all the way across the other side of the world to a jade one.

Gerald came and introduced himself to me. This was an odd meeting for me and perhaps for him also. Gerald was Sofia's teacher at high school and I was her tutor. I wondered whether he would be hostile and consider my involvement a trespass on his territory, but once again I needn't have worried so much.

Gerald spoke beautifully. The way his accent transformed words fit completely with his somewhat eccentric appearance and made listening to him all the more pleasurable. He thanked me for the help I had been giving Sofia and commented on how far ahead of the class she was.

"It's all her work!" I exclaimed, keen to let him know that Sofia had not been palming her homework off on me while she sat watching TV or getting up to whatever unmentionable mischief passed for fun among teenage Taiwanese girls. Gerald nodded, "Oh I know it is. Her style is unmistakable."

"Listen Gerald" I cut in, "I'm really struggling to understand why you've assigned them Elliot. I mean The Wasteland for Chinese kids?"

"Well you see that assignment is only for Sofia, for extra credit" he replied.

"I know it's extremely tough, but I'm having trouble with her to be honest. She's getting bored in class. She's completely unchallenged by the regular curriculum and knowing that she had a tutor I thought I'd take a risk at something that might really push her along."

I sat there and my head dropped in shame. Sofia was indeed an exceptionally gifted student and my only thought had been that I would be getting an easy ride as her tutor. I looked back at Gerald.

"Understood!" I said. "We'll get working on it at our next session on Friday evening."

"There's no great rush" said Gerald, "the project runs till the end of the year."

We spent the rest of the evening in conversation in English with Sofia and her group of classmates. If Gerald spoke any Chinese he did not let on.

After dinner Gerald left first, excusing himself as he had work to complete before the morning, he bid us all a good night and went to get his shoes. As I watched him, he pulled a green flat cap over his balding head and just as he stepped out of the door, he lifted a walking stick from where it had been thrust into a bunch of umbrellas.

I laughed out loud, wondering what forces had brought a leprechaun so far from home and drawing confused looks from Sofia and her classmates.

I spent most of my free time on Thursday and Friday reading The Wasteland and trying to come up with some way that I could help Sofia get into it, so that she could make a start on her project.

Part of me wondered why Gerald wasn't doing this, but then I recalled that the only reason there was a market for tutors in Taiwan was that class sizes were huge. It was already somewhat out of the ordinary for him to assign her extra credit work, as the system seemed to be designed to churn out perfect specimens of students, clones of some educator's ideal notion of what prospective university graduates should be, in their tens of thousands.

As it turned out, Sofia didn't turn up for her session that Friday evening, having been invited at short notice to an event in Kaohsiung, which is a city quite some way from Taipei, lying towards the southern end of Taiwan.

When Saturday came I arrived at the park just before five, to an approving look from Mr Tsai, who looked like he had already been there for some time. Mr Tsai was working through a Taiji form, a flowing sequence of movements which exercised the physical body while also awakening the internal energy.

It could easily be taken as no more than a slow motion dance, but I knew that every movement carried within it some definite martial intent, be that a defence, an attack or an evasion. Peng had once commented to me that without an understanding of the intent of the movement, one could not hope to perform it correctly and that even if the external appearance was perfect, if the intent was wrong the whole movement was wrong.

As I watched Mr Tsai I attempted to puzzle out the meaning of some of the movements. The very slow pace with which Mr Tsai performed his routine meant that it was easy to see the postures that he took and the way that one flowed into the next, but the subtlety of the movements meant that deciphering their meaning from his solo practice was mostly beyond me.

Occasionally though, a movement he made would remind me of something I had seen while practicing tui-shou and in those moments the intent was as clear as if I were watching a street performer mime riding his bicycle.

Standing there and watching him, I could feel that my body was making tiny movements and I realized that I was covertly copying his movements by doing tiny echoes of them.

A tap on the shoulder made me jump, "What are you doing?" enquired Peng.
"Just watching Mr Tsai" I replied.
"I've never seen him practicing his whole form before. It's amazing to see."
"Doing a bit more than watching I think," Peng replied.
"Are you interested in learning that form?" I wasn't really

sure how to reply. I enjoyed watching Mr Tsai's Taiji but didn't know if I wanted to learn it.

"That's ok" Peng said, "You are still looking for the right fit for you. Perhaps when you see my form you will at least have two different flavours to choose from. Come, let's cross hands." With that he drew me into the practice area and proceeded to introduce me to a much more vigorous application of his shaking fist.

I spent Saturday evening quietly, reading bits and pieces from books and playing chess with a newcomer in the tea house. I went to my room early intending to meditate but found myself distracted and only able to think about the next morning. I sat and read for a while longer and finally went to sleep.

I dreamed that night that I was Merlin, standing on the edge of a cliff and calling to the dragon and seeing not one but two dragons in the sky, coiling about one another as they chased the moon and sun through a black night full of stars.

When I arrived at the park on Sunday morning, Shun Yuan was there with Peng and Mr Tsai and an Englishman who introduced himself as Paul. Paul was quite a tall man and not slightly built, but when he began performing his form he moved with the same gentle grace as Mr Tsai.

Some of his movements looked like those that Mr Tsai did in his art, but appeared shrunken down to minimal versions of themselves.

"There's just one thing" Shun Yuan said to me quietly with a tap on the shoulder, speaking as if we had been in the middle of a conversation which had just been interrupted for seconds as opposed to the whole week.

"I can't promise to show you the same method again. What you see today will be appropriate for the circumstances, ok?" I was nodding understanding when I saw another man walking towards our group. He wore cream coloured casual trousers and jacket and was smoking a cigarette as he walked straight over the boundary of the practice area and right up to us.

His gait was so deliberately shouting nonchalance that I wondered what it was actually hiding. None of the others bat an eyelid at this, so I decided it wasn't my place to make an issue of his uninvited entrance.

Paul stopped his form and Peng turned to the man and welcomed him, but it turned out he didn't speak any Chinese and I was nominated to be their interpreter. Peng's English skills had obviously fled him that morning.

The man's name was Wayne and he was American. When I relayed Peng's question about whether he practised Taiji he replied, "For fifteen years" which came out along with a big breath of smoke and was punctuated by his flicking his cigarette butt out of his hand and onto the floor of the practice area.

I noticed the tiniest of looks dart between Peng and Shun Yuan. Then they both turned to back to Paul and apologized for having disrupted his performance and asked him to carry on. Paul fished off his demonstration and there was some discussion between the other members of the group, mostly commenting on tiny technical details of the form which were completely lost on me.

Then at one point Wayne spoke up loudly proclaiming "That's wrong. That's not correct form. Your body is all leaning over when it should be straight. Your arms are too close to your body. This isn't Taiji at all!"

Paul began trying to explain that the style of Taiji which he practised was indeed very different to the more commonly practised style, which conformed to the ideals that Wayne was describing. Wayne however was having none of it and stepping closer to Paul he said "It's not just different. It's wrong."

Shun Yuan stepped directly in front of Wayne.
"Allow me to demonstrate" he said and raised his arms in front of his body in a defensive posture.
"This is the kind of structure you are used to," he said.
"All the curves in my body are large and open. Would you like to test this structure?" Wayne shook his head and Shun Yuan altered his posture, so that the shapes of his arms became much more like Paul's had been.
"This is the same posture" he explained, "Just expressed through a different form called the small circle."

Wayne had continued shaking his head the whole time and when Shun Yuan invited him again to test his posture, he did so by pressing against Shun Yuan's defensive arms. Shun Yuan stood motionless as Wayne began to push harder and harder, changing his stance to get more leverage behind his push and clearly exerting himself now. Shun Yuan remained motionless and said, "Look Wayne. What's happened to your fifteen years of Taiji? Look how you are struggling with all your force to try and drive home a point and for what? Is it just to make our new friend look bad?"
"I'm not trying with all my force," Wayne replied.
"If I was..." and then mid-sentence without any warning and clearly intending to catch Shun Yuan off-guard, Wayne gave an almighty shove.

Shun Yuan hardly moved. He turned about his own centre and I think I saw his weight shift slightly from one foot to the other.

Wayne went flying. He tumbled right through the space where he had expected Shun Yuan to be, then caught his foot on the raised boundary of the practice area and tripped, falling head-first towards the nearest stone bench.

He caught himself on his arms and avoided serious injury and as he was picking himself up, Shun Yuan looked me right in the eye with a questioning look on his face. I nodded in reply. This time the lesson had indeed been obvious. Wayne had done this entirely to himself.

When Shun Yuan had previously given me a demonstration, I had been too closely involved to be able to see. I asked him, "Are you just a catalyst for the inevitable then?"

"I like the description" he said, "but I'm not even that. Maybe I'm just a space for the inevitable to happen."

Wayne was standing by us and was transformed.
"How did you do that?" he asked. "Could you teach me that?"

"What was that I was just saying about space for the inevitable?" Shun Yuan said, still looking directly into my eyes. I grit my teeth and tried to suppress the smile that I could feel coming.

Wayne looked on like a puppy waiting for a treat, but at that minute the group as one turned and walked out of the practice area to Peng's loud announcement in English "Breakfast!"

As we made our way out of the park and through the streets to Peng's favourite breakfast place, I kept looking back to see Wayne tagging along behind. Gone was the casual saunter with which he had approached the group. He now looked like he was hopping or skipping along and the newly lit cigarette hanging from his mouth bounced up and down and dropped ash all down his front as he did so. We arrived at the breakfast place and as we went in to sit down, Shun Yuan turned to face Wayne.

"I'd really rather you didn't smoke" he said.

"Oh of course, not while you are all eating breakfast no" Wayne replied, tossing the half-smoked cigarette on the floor. Shun Yuan looked at the cigarette butt and then back at Wayne and said, "Actually I meant not at all Wayne. I just can't take you seriously while you commit slow motion suicide in front of my face and I think that if I could see through the smoke screen I might really enjoy being able to talk to you."

Something in this touched Wayne and he reached into his pocket, took out a packet of cigarettes and threw them in the waste bin.

"Think very hard about what you want and when you are absolutely sure, go here." Shun Yuan scribbled something on a sheet of paper and with that he turned and hustled me inside to have breakfast, leaving Wayne to turn and walk off alone.

As we sat squished together at a table made for half our number and ate our breakfast, Shun Yuan sitting opposite me asked me what I had made of the events of the morning.

I was in the middle of explaining my realization that Wayne had thrown himself, going into some detail about using his force when overextended, when Peng who was sitting at my right elbow, poked me in the ribs and asked me to pass some sugar.

I reached across the table to get the sugar and Shun Yuan's finger shot out and pressed my outstretched hand against the table top.

"If you can lift it straight up again" he said, "breakfast is on me. Otherwise you buy for everyone."

Stretched as I was over the table I simply couldn't lift my hand up against the pressure of his single finger and the lesson was drummed home yet again, much to the delight of the rest of the group.

As I resorted to sliding and wriggling my hand out from under his finger I thought of complaining that the game was rigged; I had never seen anyone ask Shun Yuan for money in payment for anything. He sat there smiling at me, apparently happy to have been gifted another opportunity to show me that these lessons I was learning were deeply embedded in every minute of our lives.

"Now if you had been paying attention when I tried to explain Morphy" began Shun Yuan.

"No, no Morphy!" exclaimed Peng, waving his hands in front of his face and pulling a ridiculous expression.

It was at that moment that I realized that my whole chemistry experiment excitement had been for nothing. These guys had known each other for a while.

Then I stopped myself and thought that I had in fact witnessed a very intriguing reaction take place and wondered if Shun Yuan had sent Wayne somewhere where he would be transformed from lead to gold.

"I had an odd dream last night" I said and shared my dream with the rest of the group.

"I remember you telling me that your Order used images of dragons to symbolize universal forces" I added.

"What is the name of your Order again?" Shun Yuan looked at me hard and said quietly in English, "I haven't ever said the name of my Order to you and you should not use that name in public places here."

He kept looking at me until he appeared satisfied that I was taking him seriously enough.

"It is very sad, but the name of the Order of which I am a member has been usurped here in Taiwan and is being used by a criminal fraternity. The name of the Order is the Heavenly Dragon Society, but for your own safety you should not ever mention that you know anything about this, especially not in Chinese."

Shun Yuan looked truly saddened as he explained this to

me and I promised solemnly to take care while in Taiwan not to make mention of it.

After breakfast Shun Yuan asked me if I would mind driving him back across town to where he was staying. We walked up to Mrs Lim's and I borrowed Sofia's scooter, thinking that I should probably save up and buy one for myself.

When we arrived Shun Yuan had me sit on the porch bench while he disappeared inside. I heard the kettle whistling after a while and a moment later he appeared with two cups of coffee.

"I don't drink coffee often" he said, "but this is much too good to miss. One of Master Hong's students brought it over from America this week."

We sat and enjoyed the coffee. It was the first cup I had had in a very long time and was delicious. As we sat I found myself desperately trying to bring to mind one of the questions that I had wanted to ask. I reached for my backpack to get my notebook out then cursed myself internally for having dropped it behind the counter at the tea house when I had popped in to get the scooter keys. I winged it.

"The things you have explained to me are so different from the way they are put in the books I have read" I started, "and the demonstrations, particularly the one today about how the principles are expressed in the martial form, have really made a point. I really want to learn more but I feel like I don't know the right questions to ask and don't want to waste your time."

"Time spent with good coffee and good company is never time wasted" he said.

"You can ask me anything you want if you think it's going to help you. There's no right and wrong about it. If a question comes to mind, just ask it."

I thought then about the different forms that I had seen Mr Tsai and English Paul practise and about the form which Peng practised, which I had not seen in its entirety but which I knew would be different again.

"Is your form more like Mr Tsai's or Paul's?" I asked.

"It might be more like Peng's but I can't tell yet as I haven't seen it all" I went on.

Shun Yuan stood up and walked out onto the grassy area by the house. I cringed as he beckoned me to come, my stomach doing a weird clenching in on itself as I remembered the previous lesson he had shown me here.

I relaxed when Shun Yuan motioned for me to sit down on a bench to one side and watched as he went through a performance of his form.

The moment he started I realized that a demonstration was the only possible answer to the question I had posed. It was impossible to say that his form was more like or unlike anything else I had ever seen. It was so completely different that drawing any comparison would be nonsensical, like saying that a mathematical proof was more like a fig than an apple.

He began slowly, walking round and round in a circle with one arm extended with his palm showing towards the centre as if he were ordering some unseen entity to stop. His gaze was fixed on his outstretched hand and as he walked round and round he started to go more and more quickly.

Then a series of movements came in quick succession as he span around, rose up on one leg, swooped down low, struck out in all directions and turned clockwise and counter-clockwise, after each burst of movement returning always to the circle to follow it around until the next explosive set of changes happened.

Time seemed to stand still for me, transfixed as I was by

the beautiful complexity of the form and the intense energy with which Shun Yuan performed it.

When he had finished he stopped and stood quietly facing the centre of the circle, a thick column of steam rising into the air from the top of his head. He saw me looking at this and raised one hand above his head to wriggle his fingers in the steam.

Then he walked over to me and surprised me by placing his hands on my head. They were incredibly hot and I felt a strong vibration as he cupped my head in his hands, which became a deep sense of relaxation and went spreading through my body like a wave.

The sound of applause came from the porch area and looking up I saw a man who Shun Yuan told me was his host, Master Hong.

Master Hong came down and shook my hand and then hugged Shun Yuan with a great bear hug.
"Thank you for looking after the house my friend. Your Bagua has grown very powerful indeed" he said in heavily accented English.

So this was indeed Bagua as I had suspected. The internal martial art form which was based somehow on the mystical symbols called Trigrams in the Taoist classic text the I-Ching.

Shun Yuan introduced me to Master Hong as his friend and let him know I spoke Chinese, describing me as a student of the classics.

I was surprised at the strength of the conflicting emotions that rose up in me in response. I was so happy that Shun Yuan considered me his friend, yet at the same time I knew I wanted more.

I was awestruck by the beauty of the form he had performed and was still digesting the lessons, both spoken

and demonstrated, that seemed to continually pour out of him. I wanted to ask him to teach me and to call him Master, but felt like he had already forbidden me to do this and I was waiting for some sign that the time was right.
"It was beautiful, your form" I said.
"Do you think I would be able to learn it?" and "How long did it take you?" I asked him.
"I am still learning Rob" he replied.
"Well how long has it taken you to get to where you are now?" I pressed.
"Almost exactly thirty years" he said adding, "so far" with a faraway look in his eye.

Just then he sat down on the floor at my feet and pulled a small notepad from inside his robe. He freed a pen from the elastic band holding it in place and wrote.
"Here" he said, "this is for you". He tore out a sheet of paper and handed it to me. On it he had written a short poem.

Ahead lie only virgin snows
Behind none follow in my track
Called on alone by distant stars
I forge this way I call my self

I sat and looked at the poem and wondered if this was Shun Yuan's way of gently rejecting me as a student before I had even made an official approach. He had stood up now and looked down on me as I sat on the bench.
"I will share what I can with you while I'm around Rob" he said, "but I'm not sure how long that will be and when I go, I'm not sure how long it will be before I get back here again. And don't ask where I'm headed next when I leave here because I don't know yet."

Unwilling to believe that he was actually psychic; I told myself that he was exceptionally skilled in reading my face rather than my mind.

"Can you tell me something about your form, your Bagua?" I asked.
"Is this a practice which is taught in your Taoist Order?" Shun Yuan was holding up his hands and called out "Wait wait, slow down Robert before you leap so far over a chasm of assumption that I won't be able to catch you before you fall to your doom!"

Master Hong called to us from the house, inviting us to come in and eat something; I hadn't even noticed him move away.
"Yes, let's talk over food" agreed Shun Yuan.
"Master Hong makes amazing noodle soup and we might even talk him into brewing up a pot of his special tea." Master Hong smiled at this and we all went in and sat at his large round dinner table, which I thought could comfortably sit ten or twelve people.

I looked around the room while we waited for Master Hong to finish preparing the meal, which after triple checking my watch turned out to be a very late lunch or an early dinner. I had no clear idea of how long Shun Yuan had been performing his circling and was still not used to the way that time had recently taking to bending and warping, leaving me frequently unable to guess the hour of the day.

At that moment I felt very odd, to be sitting at a table in a distant land being served food by a Master of, what exactly? The thought dropped off as I realized I had no idea what art Master Hong was versed in. I asked Shun Yuan and he said that Master Hong practiced a system known as "Hsing-Yi", which meant form and intent.

He was also a Master of several ancient Chinese weapons and examples of these stood in racks or hung from the wall all around the room except for the far wall, which housed a large colourful shrine with many figures of deities on shelves and a large incense burner. A huge mound of ash had built up on and around the burner and I could see a thick bunch of incense sticks which had been freshly added pouring smoke towards the ceiling which was pitch black directly above the shrine.

Master Hong told me that his art, Hsing-Yi, had at its heart the same energies and mechanics of motion which were required for mastery of some of the weapons which he displayed. His favourite weapon he said was the heavy sabre and he invited me to take one down from the rack in which it stood. The reason for the name was immediately apparent and it was to Master Hong's great amusement to see me struggling with the huge sword.

A whistle from the kitchen saved me further embarrassment and Master Hong replaced the sabre in its rack and went to get our food; huge bowls of noodles in steaming soup.

Chapter eight.

The third method.

Forget passive resistance,

meet dynamic non-resistance.

"Where should I begin?" slurped Shun Yuan between mouthfuls of noodle soup.
"I suppose I should start out by talking about you!" With this he thrust his right forefinger at me which made me flinch and I tried to cover this by parodying a dodge to the side and mimed a parry of his pointing finger, looking mostly like something out of a kids cartoon.
"Hoy!" cried Master Hong around a mouthful of noodles and waving his chopsticks at me, "Don't mess around with Shun Yuan's one finger skill. That is no joking matter."
  I wanted to point out that it was exactly because he had once knocked me down and once pinned me helplessly to the table, each time using only a single finger, that I had been so jittery, but didn't get a chance as Shun Yuan had carried on talking.
"You like things to come in nice neat boxes Rob. This is Buddhism, this is Taoism and this is Animism and so on. You need to erase all the lines you like to draw around things or at the very least start blurring them a bit. I am not a Taoist, at least not in the way you meant it. If I were to fit any category of yours it would more likely be Buddhist, as the Order that I belong to names itself a Buddhist Order. Buddhism though is a transplanted religious philosophy and in every place that a seed of Buddhism has been nurtured, it

has grown into something quite different in appearance. The seed which grew into my Order was cultivated in an area with very strong Taoist influences and what you see is the result."

Master Hong gave a huge slurp of a particularly large tangle of noodles and said, "The colourful brocade is woven from silks of many colours" nodding to himself as he did so, although in appreciation of his own excellent cooking or in confirmation of Shun Yuan's words I couldn't tell.

"Exactly!" said Shun Yuan.

"Take the Bagua that you saw earlier. While it's true to say that I am an Adept of the Heavenly Dragon Order," this with a look to Master Hong and a casual wave of his hand dismissing any concern, "and while it's true that I'm a practitioner of Bagua, it's not true that the Bagua you saw comes from the Order. They meet in me you see? Just like Master Hong's brocade, the strands have become woven together into a single thing. This practice, this Bagua has become my way. It's the way I give expression to my understanding and not only in a performance such as you just witnessed. It's a continuous thing, an energy that is always bubbling up and seeking to be given shape; or rather because it happens to bubble up through me, I tend to give it shape." He finished with a satisfied nod at that, happy with himself for having made this correction.

"So how do the other members of your Order express their way?" I asked.

"Not to be rude" he replied, "but if you saw it now, you wouldn't be able to distinguish it from the performance I gave earlier." Seeing my confusion he added, "It's all about the intent Rob. Bagua is a martial form. The movements have a meaning and that meaning is directly applicable as a fighting method, albeit one belonging to times gone by; nobody I know can dodge bullets!"

He smiled and checked that I was following, continuing when he was happy he had not lost me.

"My brothers in the Order practise movements which are in appearance very much like those which I performed, but they have no martial intent whatsoever. Their work is all about the cultivation of energy in the body and the use of ritual and other practices to further their realization." I nodded my understanding and smiled as I noticed that Master Hong had pushed back from the table and was now lying back in his chair, rubbing his stomach which was straining at the vast quantity of noodles he had consumed.

We sat for a while then digesting our meal and listened to a CD compilation of classical Chinese music that Master Hong put on. After some time he got up and disappeared into the kitchen, returning with what looked like a small charcoal stove which he placed in the middle of his large round dining table.

Once the stove was lit, it burned with a surprising intensity and he put a huge kettle full of water on it to boil. Then, from a small drawer built in to the shrine holding his deities, he removed a paper bag which proved to be full of tea leaves. I had really become a lover of Chinese tea, enjoying the process of making it almost as much as drinking it. I was getting to know different flavours but my favourite was still Guan Yin tea. I recalled the tea that Shun Yuan had offered me, which he had said he had brought over from China for Mrs Lim and which had had such a different quality to it.

Master Hong reached into the paper bag with his fingertips and removed some leaves. The contents of the bag turned out to be a blend. In amongst leaves which appeared familiar to me, were others which were not like any tea leaves I had seen before, being much longer and with an earthy orange colour. Master Hong put the leaves in a dish on the table in front of him and after a moment, peered back into the bag and extracted some more, choosing only the normal green leaves and adding these to the amount already in the dish.

Then he transferred the portion of leaves into a teapot, small and very simple in design but with the most incredible deep red colour and an almost golden patina. This I knew to have been developed over time by very delicate care of the pot.

In Chinese the verb meaning to take care of a teapot in this way was the same verb used when talking about rearing animals and enthusiasts often talked at length about "rearing" or "cultivating" their teapots.

Master Hong's was a particularly beautiful example of the results which could be obtained, although usually only after years. I asked him how long he had had the teapot and he replied that it had been in his family for more generations than his grandfather had known when passing it down to him.

I wondered then at his making use of the pot for brewing our tea, but watching the intense delicacy with which he handled it I understood that the antiquity of the object was uppermost in his mind. I felt a strong sense of connection to ancient China then and wondered who had made the pot and who had drunk the first tea to be brewed in it.

When Master Hong was satisfied that the tea was ready, he prepared four of the tiny cups from which one drinks Chinese tea by first immersing them in hot water and then filling them with the first brew of the leaves. This was never drunk, but was poured out over the teapot to run into the bowl in which it stood. He did the same with the second brew.

Normally the third brew is the first one to be tasted, but as he poured it he said he was not happy with the colour and so this brew was also used to rinse the cups and was then poured away.

He was happy with the fourth brew and filled the four cups, placing one in front of Shun Yuan, one in front of me, keeping one for himself and placing the last at a spot on the table over to his left.

I asked him why he set the other cup aside in that manner and Shun Yuan replied smiling, "Now that he's asked, you have to tell the story."

"I don't mind" I interjected, "If you'd rather wait until afterwards."

"No there won't be a chance afterwards Robert" he said and shaking his head he stood up and retrieved a small box from the shrine. He opened the box, which was empty but for a small quantity of the orange tea leaves. The box he told me used to contain a relic; a small round white ball of matter which was removed from the ashes of an old Master after cremation. I recalled vaguely having read about such things and did my best to hide my disappointment at not being able to see one myself.

Some years before he explained, he had received a visitor and during conversation had brought out the relic. The two had sat discussing the properties of such things and Master Hong had said that one of these properties was that they were said to be indestructible. The visitor had challenged him to try and destroy the thing and being in a certain mood that day he had agreed. He had taken the relic, which from his gestures I guessed was about half the size of a golf ball and placed it on a cloth on the table and hit it with a hammer.

His guest had complained that he wasn't really trying and said that he could drop the matter if he wished to.

Master Hong had then lifted the hammer and struck down on the relic as hard as he could and the thing had disappeared. I asked him several times what he meant exactly by that and with his head in his hands he said that it had just vanished.

He had thought at first that he had pulverized the relic, but there was no sign of dust or any residue on the cloth or on the table. Then he thought that as he had struck it, he must not have caught it square on and that the relic had pinged away. Neither he nor his guest had heard it strike anything else however and turning the room upside down they had not been able to locate it.

As he told his story, Master Hong was looking around the dining room where we were sitting.
"Was it this room!?" I asked.
"Yes" he replied "and this guest who taught me one of the bitterest and most valuable lessons I have ever had" pointing to Shun Yuan.
"It was the intent you see?" he went on. "In summoning all my intent and putting all my power into destroying the thing I committed myself absolutely to my desire to smash it and in doing that I lost any connection with it, lost the right to keep hold of it. So now each time I make this tea, I leave a cup as an offering to my Great-Great-GrandMaster in the hopes that one day the relic will be returned to me."

As I sat and thought about his story, Master Hong poured away the cold teas and refreshed the little cups again. I drank my tea, savouring the powerful aroma of oranges and the sweet taste and I found myself hoping that Master Hong would indeed be reunited with his relic one day, even as I wondered how much of his story I should be taking literally.

A few moments later I stood up and saw that Shun Yuan and Master Hong had also stood up at the exact same time.

Without saying anything the three of us walked out to the grass beside the house. My body felt light and I felt full of energy.

Shun Yuan demonstrated to me how to form the circle around which I would walk and instructed me how to place my hands and where to look with my eyes. Then he set me to walking round and round my circle.

The sensations in my body grew intense and I struggled trying to grasp them with my mind, only to have them change or move as I did so. One sensation which persisted was an intense vibration which travelled continuously up the length of my spine.

Almost as quickly as it had come on, the effect, which I assumed, had come from Master Hong's tea, disappeared again. It became immediately difficult to keep up the pace at which I had just been going and I was surprised at how quickly I became exhausted from such a simple thing as walking around in a circle.

I stopped then and watched the two Masters as they practised their respective arts; the complex twisting circles of Shun Yuan's Bagua only highlighted the more by the powerful direct force of Master Hong's Hsing-Yi, which darted forwards or in zigzag bursts.

Time flew by again and at one point I absentmindedly looked at my watch to see it was getting really late. I excused myself then, saying I would have to head home and asked Shun Yuan when I would next see him.
"Oh I'll be in the park in the morning" he said. I nodded enthusiastically at this. Monday morning was my least favourite time to be in the park, due both to the lower turnout of Peng's group but also to a weirdly ingrained dislike for Mondays that I couldn't quite explain. I tended to blame the Boomtown Rats and the subliminal power of their

music if the topic ever came up in conversation.

I spent no time meditating that evening, but slept extremely well and when I awoke I recalled a dream.

In the dream I was walking with Shun Yuan along a path over a hill beside the sea and then down onto the sand. In the distance a group of young men were walking towards us. When we met, one of the young men stepped out of the group and challenged Shun Yuan to a duel. When Shun Yuan attempted to decline, the young man insisted and launched an attack at him. Shun Yuan opened his mouth and bolt of lightning hit the young man in the chest and he fell to the floor.

I got to the park in record time that Monday morning and was happy to see a great turnout. Peng was there and Shun Yuan; these two had already begun working together. Mr Tsai was there and was uncommonly talkative as he discussed the fine points of his form with English Paul. I looked around to see if Wayne had shown up, but there was no sign of him.

I turned to watch Shun Yuan and Peng working out together. They were practicing a freeform kind of tui-shou, each gently but firmly testing the balance and the root of the other. They seemed to be giving each other notes, quietly spoken as they practised and I repeatedly saw Shun Yuan shake his head slightly after Peng had made a comment. I couldn't hear well enough to know what was being said, but there appeared to be a disagreement.

To my surprise and disbelief Peng's movement suddenly exploded as he grabbed Shun Yuan by the arms and pulled him clear out of his deeply rooted stance, letting out an almighty shout as he did so. In that instant I saw a victorious look begin to emerge on Peng's face as Shun

Yuan flew forward under the force of the attack.

In the next instant Shun Yuan's palm touched Peng on the chest sending Peng flying backwards and tumbling into the dirt. Shun Yuan stood there looking down at Peng and said "That's what I was trying to say".

Peng leapt up and demanded another go and once more the two began, gently getting into a flow and feeling each other's rhythms.

Three times it happened. Peng repeated his technique and every time I was sure that he had managed it, yet somehow all that force was redirected back into him and flew off and crashed into the dirt.

The third time I was watching Shun Yuan intently, hoping to understand exactly how he had defeated Peng's shaking fist in such a manner, but it appeared he had done nothing at all. I couldn't detect anything, try as I might, that could explain how he had done it.

The next time that Peng came back, Shun Yuan refused, worried that he might harm Peng, who stood back then and announced to the group that his shaking fist had not only been dissolved, but had been turned completely against him.

A soft voice requested my attention in English then and I looked around to find myself face to face with a giant. "Gareth" he said quietly, reaching out a hand that looked like it belonged on a gorilla.

"I was wondering if you would introduce me to your friends. My Chinese is really poor though." Gareth wasn't just big, he was massive, but his softly spoken voice and the small gestures he made with his hands as he spoke immediately made him the very epitome of a gentle giant and I felt completely at ease with him. His t-shirt looked like it had been sprayed on over his muscles, which rippled as he spoke. I realized that I hadn't ever truly understood the term rippling muscles until just then.

I introduced Gareth to Shun Yuan and Peng who greeted him warmly in English, Peng hurriedly apologizing for his horrible pronunciation and Shun Yuan taking the opportunity to tease him for it.

Gareth was also a student of martial arts, but studied in a completely different style. He had come to Taiwan a few months earlier to train with his Master and hoped to stay until he was ready to go back and teach in the US. He said he normally lived some way from Taipei, down on the east coast of the country, but was in town for a few days finalizing some visa arrangements.

Peng enquired as to his teacher's name and replied with a surprised expression and a double thumbs-up when Gareth told him.

The conversation turned then and Gareth, politely acknowledging the skill of the members of the group, said that the internal arts just weren't his thing.

"I do understand the notion of passive resistance" he said, "it's just that for me, well as the saying goes back home, I'd rather have peace through superior firepower."

Peng asked if he could see some of Gareth's style and he gladly obliged, going through a form which he called "The Butterfly" but which left me more in mind of a herd of stampeding buffalo.

His movements bore some resemblance to the very direct motions that I had seen Master Hong perform, but even I could see that this was entirely different. There was an overt power here and an obvious destructive intent to almost every movement.

Gareth finished off the form and got a huge round of applause from the whole group, who had gathered around to watch while he performed the routine.

"I think this is my favourite aspect" Gareth ventured in

Mandarin and performed one single movement, a twist of his body which shot his fist out in a punch.

Just then and later on, every time I thought about that punch I found it impossible to fathom how Gareth was generating such force. I found I was not alone in this assessment as several members of the group stated quite clearly that they thought Gareth was already getting to a point where they would not be able to face his technique.

With comments coming from all over Gareth had trouble following and asked me if I would translate. When I summarized what had been said, he looked crushed and told me that he was hoping he'd be able to learn something from practitioners of the internal arts which would then allow him to improve his own, thoroughly external practice. I translated for him and asked if anyone in the group wished to work with Gareth and only Shun Yuan's voice came in reply, "Sure, why not?"

Gareth gave Shun Yuan a very formal bow and asked permission to perform his turning strike and Shun Yuan nodded assent. Space was made and I found myself nervously shifting from foot to foot as I watched from the side-lines with Peng at my side.

Shun Yuan stood in front of Gareth, his arms hanging relaxed at his sides and looked like he was a child, standing waiting in line for an ice-cream. His face had a look of open wonderment that reminded me of a tiny baby and said that he clearly had no idea what was about to happen but was excited to find out.

"Passive resistance" Shun Yuan said "was Ghandi's term. He was a pacifist, not a martial artist. Please don't be polite." This last, said with a tiny nod to Gareth was a ritualized way of giving permission for the other to use their technique to the full extent of their ability. My heart was beating in my mouth as I watched.

Gareth appeared to shrink in on himself ever so slightly as he contracted his muscles and then let leash with his technique which I was sure was significantly faster than he had performed it before and was accompanied by a shout which I thought might have deafened me had I been standing closer.

Shun Yuan had not moved an inch. My eyes widened and my mouth dropped open as I saw the strike hit him in the solar plexus.

Then I gasped out loud. As Gareth's striking hand had touched his robe, Shun Yuan's whole body had instantly spun around like a tornado. The strike encountered nothing but air and Gareth had suddenly found himself struggling to keep control of his balance.

Shun Yuan's spinning body had taken him out of the line of Gareth's attack and put him at his side and the same motion resulted in his arms flying out and his right palm slapping Gareth in the back of the head with an almighty cracking sound and a force which dropped the gentle giant to one knee.

Gareth knelt there for a moment and then stood and turned to face Shun Yuan who gave him the deepest bow I had seen yet.

"Thank you so much" Shun Yuan said.

"You took me to the limit of my ability just then and gave me the opportunity to show something real to my friend here," he continued, pointing me out.

Gareth shook Shun Yuan's hand vigorously and said that he had learned a new lesson that day and asked him if he could say something about the principle behind the technique.

"I can talk to you about principles Gareth" he replied, "but it is very difficult for me to talk to you about technique because a technique implies something preconceived, some kind of planned response to your attack. So in that sense there really was no technique involved here, only principle and that principle was dynamic non-resistance." He stopped and pointed out Peng and carried on to say, "It was the same principle just now, when you were watching my friend Peng and I practicing. His shaking fist technique is extremely strong. It's so strong that I don't have the ability to absorb it like Mr Tsai over there can, so I was left with no option but complete non-resistance. This ended up with his own force reflecting back onto him. In your case it was slightly different. You had focused all your intent down into a tiny dot here" he pointed to his solar plexus then and Gareth nodded in response saying, "The more you can focus your intent, the more power you can deliver through the technique."

"Ah" Shun Yuan breathed, "but the smaller that dot becomes, the more committed you are to your technique actually needing to find something there. If I can manage to not be where the dot is, the rest will happen by itself. So your technique contains within itself the very thing that limits it. This is exactly in accordance with Yin and Yang."

Gareth was nodding and rubbing the back of his head. The rest of the session that morning Shun Yuan spent with Gareth and I looked on, part of me feeling left out at not being able to converse or indeed take part to the same level, but another part of me feeling very fortunate to be able to experience these things at all.

I kicked myself when I got home that evening for forgetting to tell Shun Yuan about the dream. It had now taken on an almost prophetic quality in my mind and as I sat writing in my journal I thought back to the dream and then to the session in the park and the obvious parallels and wondered at the ability of the mind to pull such amazing stunts.

I kicked myself again when I realized that I had not made any arrangements for when I would next meet Shun Yuan and wondered if he would turn up at the park in the morning.

As I knelt in meditation that night, I found myself once again becoming utterly still and feeling deeply peaceful as the wave of warmth flowed down over my head and body. My mind was full of the images of the day and when I slept that night my dreams were incredibly energetic yet disappeared from memory the moment I woke.

Chapter nine.

The fourth method.

A blinding flash. Blinding stupidity.

I didn't see Shun Yuan for the rest of the week. He wasn't in the park in the mornings, he didn't come to the tea house and the one time that I drove out to Master Hong's neither of them were there.

To add to this, when I came down from my room one morning I realized that Mrs Lim and Sofia were also absent and learned from Morning later in the day that they were now both in Kaohsiung. In answer to my questions about why they had gone, she replied with a downturned mouth and a shoulder shrug, holding her palms up to show empty hands and saying "I don't know" but pronouncing only the vowels and all blended together so the sound came out as "Iuhoh." Even as I wondered where this horrible affectation came from, I found myself marvelling once more at the powers of mimicry possessed by Taiwanese students and thought it ultimately had to come down to the language.

Chinese is a tonal language, where two words with the exact same phonetic structure mean entirely different things when they are spoken in different tones, this giving rise to countless jokes and puns, thankfully not all of these directed at defenceless foreigners.

Tonality was so embedded in their minds that whenever Morning or Swift or Little Rabbit asked me to tell them a new word in English and repeated it back to me, it was as if I was hearing myself speak, their repetition perfectly capturing not only the basic form of the word, but also the exact intonation that I had applied to it. It was a struggle getting them to understand that tones did not have the same meaning in English and I wondered what life would be like, if indeed English words had this quality. I imagined myself to be back in my grandmother's kitchen as a little child, pointing at the dog and complaining to her that the bamboo basket had stolen my sandwich.

I took to more wandering around the park in the mornings and it was on the Thursday of that week while I was exploring a corner of the park that I hadn't spent any time in before, that I first saw Honey.

Honey was instantly captivating, not only the most delicious eye-candy but a martial artist to boot! She was performing a routine with double swords, a whirling blur of movement that I found highly reminiscent of Shun Yuan's Bagua but with a far more gymnastic flavour.

While Shun Yuan's movement was deeply rooted in the ground, she leapt in the air and spun or kicked, turned somersaults and displayed a range of motion unlike anything I else I had ever seen, unless perhaps a ballet dancer. She dropped into and rose out of the splits several times during the routine showing the same ease with which I scratch my nose.

Her long jet black hair, bound up in a braid which reached all the way down her back when she was still, flew this way and that throughout her performance, causing the metallic hairband attached to the end of the braid to dart about like it was a third weapon.

At one point the braid must have come loose because her hair escaped, transforming the single black rope into a wild spray that shot out from her head in all directions and gave her an unearthly look, like a witch riding on a storm. This brought the routine to a sudden stop and sheathing her swords, Honey sat down to attend to her hair.

I just had to say something to her, to show my appreciation for the display of skill I was telling myself, but how do you approach a beautiful woman who is also an expert with the sword and say anything without it appearing like you are hitting on her and getting chopped to bits? This was especially worrisome for me as at least seventy per cent of my mind was drooling at the possibilities implied by such wonderful flexibility.

I stood there entirely wrapped up in a bubble of fantasy, watching her trying to tame her hair which seemed to have taken on a life of its own. Then the bubble popped as Honey's girlfriend came and sat next to her on the bench. Overt shows of affection are not the norm in Taiwan, in my experience particularly not among gay and lesbian couples, but I recognized instantly that they were indeed a couple and so, released from the spell of my fantasizing I was able to walk over and say hello.

Honey smiled in thanks at my enthusiastic praise of her form, a smile that would melt a glacier and after querying me about my own studies she took me to meet her Master. Old Li, as everyone called him, did not look old at all and despite my efforts to drop my useless notions and expectations I found myself shocked once again when he told me he was seventy five.

I had estimated him to be in his forties and that was when I became absolutely convinced that the Chinese had in fact found the secret of longevity in these arts of theirs. I thought back to old tales from Chinese literature describing immortals and thought that if a person were able to reach one hundred back then, when life expectancies were so much shorter, they would probably have seemed like an immortal to those around them.

Old Li was an immigrant from the mainland he told me, where he had studied Chinese medicine, Taiji, calligraphy and music from his Master before being swept up in the turmoil of the Cultural Revolution and finding himself one of many seeking refuge in Taiwan.

Honey got up to leave with her girlfriend and I watched them go, at first thinking that the feeling coming over me was a yearning for the unattainable, but then realizing that it was the simple desire for the warm company of a lover.

I thought that whatever the rain gods of Taiwan were doing, it wasn't doing anything for the drought I found myself in.

Old Li clapped me on the back and invited me to walk with him around the park. He seemed to know everyone and they all called out to him as we passed and I felt as if I was walking around with royalty. Old Li had a deep appreciation for all the arts that we saw as we walked, commenting on the history of the systems and pointing out subtle differences in form which he told me distinguished a student as being from one school or another.

"Sometimes I worry" he said, "that these arts will die out in a couple of generations" and then he went on to tell me the story of the young village fool who sat and starved in an orchard because he couldn't decide which fruit he wanted to pick and eat.

In the tea house that evening as I sat writing in my journal and drinking "Pu Er" tea, I looked up to see Morning walking by and suddenly thought that Old Li had been referring to me as the young fool in the orchard. He had probably seen me drooling over Honey; I'd been staring for long enough.

I thought then that I was really a fool and that my so-called drought was entirely self-imposed. I got to thinking about the girls working in the tea house, but pretty as they were there was no spark, no connection of the intimate kind with them.

I was surprised then, when on the Saturday morning of that week, Morning said that she wanted to accompany me on my shopping trip. I didn't really know what to make of her self-invitation but thought that if she wanted to tag along that would be fine. I needed to buy myself a new cover for my comforter, something like a mattress on which I slept; there was no bed in my room and sleeping directly on the tatamis was too uncomfortable.

We spent some time walking around the shops and I found one which sold covers with colourful cartoons printed on them which made me grin. Searching through the collection I found one, yellow with a gigantic picture of Snoopy laying on top of his doghouse and proclaiming, "I think I'm allergic to mornings."

I snorted a laugh as I read it and thought I had to have it, quickly paying for it and stuffing it into the bag before my companion caught sight of it. This was a joke which would have to remain completely private.

We had a really nice day then, having lunch together and wandering slowly around as Morning showed me Taipei through her eyes. As we walked and talked we fell into a casual ease with each other. I realized after a while that I did consider her a friend but that there was no chance of anything else growing between us. Morning's life was full of movie stars and pop music, clothes shopping and gossip magazines. As delightful as she could be, there was nothing apart from the fact that she worked at the tea shop and had a desire to improve her English that connected us. I grew resigned to the drought lasting a bit longer and reminded myself to enjoy the platonic company of my friends.

When we got back I went to my room and removed the old cover from my comforter, replacing it with the colourful new Snoopy one and enjoyed another private laugh at the joke.

I went out to eat that evening, having been overcome with a desire to go back to the Noodle Paradise. Perhaps I would even see Shun Yuan there I thought.

The Li brothers were in fine form, joking with their guests and showing off their skills at every opportunity. The noodles were as incredible as I remembered them and I sat through two large bowls and then gave a large sigh of satisfaction as I slumped back in the chair, utterly replete. I sat there for a good long time, enjoying cups of tea and chatting with Older Li, all the while hoping that Shun Yuan would walk in the door.

Eventually I figured he wasn't going to show up and with that I decided to head back to the tea house and go up to bed.

As I came in through the front door of the tea house a raised girl's voice came ringing out angrily from the staff area, "Tao Yen!" and Morning came storming out from behind the bar and then exited through the side door to the tea house, slamming it shut behind her as she went.

I walked into the staff area where Swift and Little Rabbit were sitting at the table eating and was shredded by the black looks full of daggers that they cast my way. Morning's food was still at her place mostly untouched and on the table beside her bowl was a Chinese-English dictionary. "Tao Yen" is Chinese for despicable and that was exactly how I felt when I picked up the dictionary which was lying open at the entry for "allergic".

I had put my foot squarely and deeply in it and as I shrank away I wondered how I was ever going to redeem myself. Meditation eluded me that night and trying to sleep early also failed, leaving me to sit awake in my room and choke on my own idiocy.

I woke early on the Sunday and tried to put Morning's angry reaction out of my mind but with no success. It seemed to me like a bit of an overreaction to what was after all nothing but a harmless accident of a pun.

The part of my mind that remembered laughing at her expense was quickly and mercilessly silenced by my insistence that this was an innocent mistake, until a moment later it struck back at me and wondered how Morning had known what was printed on the cover of my comforter.

There was no way she could have seen it in the shop, of that I was absolutely sure. She had not been anywhere near me when I'd picked it up. In fact she had been on the other side of the shop and I had walked over to her after I had paid and the cover was securely in my bag.

I didn't want to go where my mind was leading me, but just as in a horror film or a nightmare, I found myself drawn along down the dark path as I realized that she had been in my room. Adding to my torture my mind asked what she had been doing there. In particular why she had been anywhere near where I slept, which was in the far corner from the door.

I swallowed hard as I asked myself if she had gone to my room to wait for me and had sat down on my comforter, then become curious about the slogan which included her name. A terrible sense of cold came over me then, a feeling that I had committed a serious offence of karma and would surely be severely punished for it.

I had to snap myself out of it and double-timed all the way to the park, where I hoped at least a sound thrashing by my friends would be penance enough. Deep within I knew I was kidding myself.

When I arrived at the park it was busier than ever. Groups everywhere seemed to be at maximum capacity and Peng's group was no exception, with all the old members present and many new faces that had come along to join in.

Peng took me around, introducing me to so many people that I had no chance of remembering anyone's name until we met Wu Feng.

Wu Feng was in his twenties and tall for a Chinese. He was also well built, having the same kind of muscular look that Gareth had had, but without the huge bulk. As I shook his hand I couldn't help noticing their condition. His palms were roughly calloused and his knuckles huge. His fingers looked powerful and I was convinced that had he wished to do so, he could have crushed my hand in his grip.

Wu Feng noticed me noticing his hands and this started off a discussion on hand conditioning exercises and the very different approaches taken by different schools. Wu Feng walked over to one of the trees in the practice area and demonstrated the results of his conditioning by striking hard at the tree, which made me wince as I felt sure he must have broken something. He was of course unhurt and talked at some length about the special medicinal preparations that were an essential part of developing the hands into weapons.

Several folks agreed that it was getting more and more difficult to find the genuine article and Wu Feng offered to introduce them to his Master, who brewed the special ointment that he used.

Just then Shun Yuan arrived and Peng introduced him to Wu Feng. I walked up to Shun Yuan and said, "Give me your hands", reaching out my hands in a demanding emphasis to my request. Shun Yuan held his hands out and I took them in mine. He had small hands I saw again, now noting that they were also free of callouses and that his knuckles were not at all pronounced.

"Wu Feng has been talking to us about hand conditioning," I went on.

"What kind of hand conditioning do you practice? Your hands are like a child's compared to his." Shun Yuan replied by poking out his tongue and then saying, "The soft endures, the hard withers utterly away. Any toothless old man can tell you this."

"But how do you do your one finger skill without damaging yourself?" I persisted, this question drawing a disbelieving sound from Wu Feng.

"Hoy! Don't underestimate the power of Shun Yuan's one finger skill" I said, doing my best impression of Master Hong.

Wu Feng looked at Shun Yuan and said directly, "You do not have one finger skill" to which Shun Yuan replied, "Please don't take this badly, but my one finger skill has nothing to do with being able to do a handstand on one finger, or being able to drive your fingers through a coconut or any other such method."

"Then please demonstrate" said Wu Feng, "exactly what is meant by your one finger skill." With this he stepped away to an open space in the practice area and took up a stance which was clearly a fighting position.

My mind kept saying "But, but, but" over and over and as I watched Shun Yuan walk over to face Wu Feng, I felt once again like a stupid child, this time one who had ruined the picnic by stirring up a hornet's nest with a stick.

"Do not be polite" said Wu Feng, in the ritualized call to an opponent to show his best skill, continuing then, "I will not hold back my hand." With that he took a step towards Shun Yuan, his hands making circles in front of him which gradually claimed the empty space between them.

Shun Yuan's posture appeared to shrink in on itself and

his right arm took on a very strange coiled shape, tucked under his right armpit. Wu Feng moved forwards and his own posture became more expansive. He threw a punch at Shun Yuan's head and in that same moment, as Shun Yuan's head ducked away his coiled right arm shot out like a cracking whip and the tip of his middle finger struck Wu Feng on the eye. Wu Feng screamed out as he fell to his knees, his hands covering his face as he shouted, "Blinding light! I can't see, I can't see!" the panic in his voice obvious to all there.

Shun Yuan knelt immediately beside him and put his arm around his shoulder and said, "Keep your eyes closed and relax. It is temporary. Your optic nerve has taken a bad shock and fired strong signals to your brain which can only be interpreted as blinding light. Move your eyes around in their sockets while you keep them closed. Those painful white flashes you see have already started to subside yes?" Wu Feng nodded at this and Shun Yuan told him to remove his hands from his face and slowly open his eyes. As his face came into view once more I could see a livid red arc on the lower lid of his left eye, the exact shape of the curve of Shun Yuan's middle fingernail.

"Dart fingers" said Wu Feng. "Are you a student of Wing Chun?"

"No" replied Shun Yuan.

"My one finger skill comes simply from Yin and Yang theory. I have never studied Wing Chun."

"What's Wing Chun?" I asked, having not heard the name before and Peng told me that it was a style of martial art of which one of the forms was called "Dart Fingers" and which emphasized such blindingly fast striking movements.

"I really need to cut my nails" said Shun Yuan looking at his hand and then at Wu Feng as if the comment was made in apology. The two bowed formally and then shook hands and I realized that I had once again witnessed a scene which roused in me a deep sense of connectedness to ancient China.

Despite what had just happened, there was no tension, no hint of animosity between these two men who were now chatting as if they had known each for years.
"My way is simple" Shun Yuan said to me then.
"The hard meets the soft" he explained, touching his fingernail against his eyelid.
"The soft meets the hard" this time showing his open palm and placing it against the side of his head.
"These things happen in accordance to what is appropriate for the moment."

Inspired by this I walked over and picked up a small paving slab which lay just outside the practice area where it had come loose and said "can you break this? Can you show me what is appropriate in this case?"

Shun Yuan nodded and took the paving slab, hefting it in his left hand and considering, before dropping it to the floor where it broke in two. I couldn't conceal the look of disappointment which came over my face and in response Shun Yuan said quietly, "You must be exhausted if you are still carrying that bag of expectations around." Then driving his message home further he carried on, "Rob, if you can't put aside your expectations and preconceptions, how are you going to have any authentic experience?"

For some reason my mind went immediately to how I had upset Morning and I said, "I've hurt someone with my stupid preconceptions and my childishness and I really need some help to fix it. Please help me."

We walked together then and I explained what had happened and how I had no idea what I should do next to make things better. We went to cross the street and as Shun Yuan stepped off the kerb he froze there with one foot hovering and said, "I have no idea what I am doing next Rob" and remained stopped there on one leg at the side of the road, looking across to the breakfast place which I had supposed was our destination.

"I am aware of myself here and now" he said "but next? I can look across the street and decide I am going over there and then suddenly be distracted by a face looking at me out of a bus window, or an old friend's long unheard voice calling out to me and the Way suddenly whisks me off and breakfast is forgotten."

I looked at him then and he read my expression to mean I was hungry and said, "Don't worry, not this time" and strode across the street.

"Is it lonely?" I asked, "Living life in such a way." He looked at me with a look of absolute confusion and shook his head. "How could it possibly be lonely when I'm surrounded by friends?" he asked.

"But they are all only temporary right? At some point the Way is going to whisk you off somewhere else and you won't be around your friends anymore." Shun Yuan pulled an empty plastic bottle from inside his robe and knocked me on the head with it before depositing it in the waste bin outside the breakfast place.

"So the friends are temporary" he mused, "but the being whisked away from them is permanent?" He looked at me genuinely expecting a reply and I could only look back dumbly.

"You have to face the music obviously Rob. Don't try to duck out of it, just go back there and say sorry and leave yourself open to whatever happens. Don't try to defend a single shred of your ego by explanations and qualifications. Invest in loss Rob and understand that your redemption will only appear in the uttermost depths of your defeat. Just hope that you are conscious enough to know what's going on when she's done with you."

With that he turned and walked off down the street, leaving me standing outside the breakfast place to choose between my growling stomach and continuing a conversation. I cursed myself at that. Of course the choice I should be making was between satisfying my hunger and going back immediately to apologize to Morning. It was with this realization that I too turned away from the breakfast place and started walking home.

Morning wasn't there when I got to the tea house, but the moment she arrived I walked up to her and apologized for having upset her.

It all came out as one long blurt. I told her I was sincerely sorry for having hurt her and said how much I valued her as a friend. I said that I deeply regretted totally misreading the situation and had had no idea that she had any feelings for me at all, let alone those kinds of feelings.

As Morning looked at me her face turned scarlet red and she slapped me hard, turned on her heel and stormed off. Holding my stinging face and feeling even more confused by what had happened I walked into the staff area in a daze and sat down.

Swift was there reading a magazine and I asked her "Do you know what Morning was doing in my room the other day?"
"Saturday" she replied without looking up, as if the single word were more than enough explanation, then adding "She has to mop the floors on Saturdays remember?"
"Mop the floors" I repeatedly stupidly as I felt myself falling further and further down the hole I had been busy digging.

Chapter ten.

The fifth method.

Playing the lute, ringing in the bells.

"What were you thinking?" asked Shun Yuan over his teacup. I had driven out to Master Hong's house later that evening in the hopes of finding him and when I did so he had claimed to be starving.

We had gone together then down to a local night market. Set up on both sides of the street and running the entire length it boasted stalls selling everything imaginable, from underpants to laptops, but Shun Yuan only had eyes for the food section at the far end.

We ambled along stopping at this stall and that to enjoy the incredible range of dishes that were on offer, many completely new to me. Eating out late at night by the side of the road was not something that had initially struck me as all that appealing, but the Taiwanese had it down to a true art form.

I had thought that so many different cooks working in such close confines would have created a terrible smell, with odours of different dishes clashing, but somehow the smells from all the different stalls came together in a tantalizing harmony and I felt like a cartoon dog, lifted off the ground, his nose pulled along by a wisp of delicious smoke curling out from a forbidden pie.

"I don't know" I replied, refilling my cup.
"I guess I'm trying to get my thick-head skill to the level of your one finger skill." Shun Yuan wasn't impressed with this and let me know it with a pursing of his lips.

"You leapt from one set of assumptions earlier on, across the entire range of possibilities to the extreme opposite assumption and thrust that right in her face! It's not good enough Rob. You owe it to this girl to at least learn something from the experience. She's not like these folks you've seen in the park. Whether pushed on by their ego and a need to be right, or drawn on by their sincere desire to improve, all those folks make a conscious choice to come to the practice area and go through a learning experience. Morning was just an innocent bystander and you bitch-slapped her with the consequences of poor decision making and lack of sensitivity. So I ask you again, what were you thinking? You asked me for help, were the instructions not clear enough?"

He sat there looking at me then as he munched on a spoonful of some condiment or other, letting out a high pitched "mmm" and immediately spooning out some more.

I felt like a little child getting scolded by his parents and shook my head as I replied, "I really don't know. I walked up to her, said sorry and…"

"Why is there an 'and' at the end there?" his question coming with a sharp chopping gesture of his had cut me off, before he then returned to his spoon to his mouth.

I thought about it and my mind turned to treacle. I found it extraordinarily difficult to focus on this and found myself getting frustrated. The instruction had been simple enough, say sorry and then be quiet and allow her to let rip, yet from somewhere this whole mess had blurted out uncontrolled.

"I think" he mumbled around another spoonful, "that I know where the issue is. I think I can help you move forward, but first you just have to try this, it's just amazing!" and with that he thrust a spoonful of some yellowish-green substance at my face and I opened my mouth and chewed reflexively.

The pain was instantaneous; a burning so intense that my face went immediately bright red, my eyes watered and my whole body became drenched in sweat.

I grabbed instinctively for my glass of water, wanting to douse the fire in my mouth, but Shun Yuan grabbed me by the wrist and said "That isn't going to help you Rob. Water will do nothing to ease this. In fact it's only going to spread the burning to every corner of your mouth and down your throat. That lemon is what you need."

He reached over to a basket of small greenish lemons at the end of the table and placed one in front of me, all the while holding my right wrist in a vice like grip which I knew I could not escape from.

I seized up. My whole body was tense as I put all my effort into escaping his grip so that I could reach over for the water which I knew I needed. I didn't know why I didn't believe him, I didn't have any specific reason to doubt that the lemon would help my burning mouth, but I feared that I would bite down on it and be catapulted into some new universe of agony as Shun Yuan broke into hysterical laughter.

This brought me to my senses. Strange indeed he was, but I had never seen him cruel and with my free hand I picked up the lemon and bit into it. The relief was immediate; the juice of the lemon neutralizing the effect of what I thought must have been chilli in the sauce he had fed me.

As I relaxed he let my wrist go and said "There is a core in the middle of you, an incredibly strong and compact core which holds on to your ideas about yourself and the world around you and does everything it can to defend itself. I can help you Rob, but you are really not going to like it. I keep talking to you about investing in loss, but you have been investing in something else altogether. You have to stop your meditation and breathing work immediately and until I advise you to start again."

This shocked me and I shook my head at him and asked, "But why? I really feel like I've been getting somewhere with it."

"That's the problem Rob" he replied.

"When we first met you said that you wanted to learn about the Tao in your everyday life, but what you have done is keep your meditation practice apart from your everyday life. You do the same thing with the sessions in the park" he added.

Inside I heard myself shouting out how Peng had said I was doing so well, how I'd managed to demonstrate a real understanding of what he had been teaching. He'd gone out of his way to show me where others were failing where I had succeeded.

"All the progress you think you are making, all the learning you think you are doing, is simply fuelling that inner core. We need to get Rob out of the way so that you can see the Tao happening from moment to moment. There are several ways to do this; one of them is called 'eating bitter'."

"Could we perhaps consider another way?" I asked in a pleading tone, my mouth still full of memories of fire and brimstone.

He was shaking his head then, "We'll try this first as it has the best chance of getting you somewhere in a relatively short time. Then we can move on to something else."

I sat there contemplating what I was about to let myself in for and then said, "Ok teacher, when do we start?" He looked at me a long while then, before finally nodding and replying, "We'll stick with the park for now, it has a good energy and I think we can accomplish something with that method if we do it the right way. Meet me there at 5." With that he got up and left me sitting there, wondering if I had just apprenticed myself to a demon.

By the time I got back to the tea shop I only managed a fitful couple of hours sleep before it was time to get up and head down to the park.

Shun Yuan was there when I arrived and I watched as he completed a performance of his form to the appreciative murmurs of a group of onlookers. He came to greet me and we went together then.

He stood right in the middle of Peng's practice area and just as Peng had done, he drew a circle on the earth around his feet and said "remove me from the circle. You may use your right hand only."

I stood in front of him and pushed at his chest with my right hand and felt no resistance as he melted away. The next moment I felt his left hand cuff me around the right ear.

"Again" he said. I pushed once more and again felt my push simply expanding out into nothingness as Shun Yuan shifted his weight slightly. A moment later his left hand cuffed me around the right ear again.

I was distracted by some of the other members of Peng's group arriving and decided that I needed to make a good showing. I changed my stance and pushed again at Shun Yuan's chest, this time his left hand cuffing my ear caused me to stumble slightly and I decided to reject that stance and returned to my original standing posture.

Shun Yuan stood there, motionless and expressionless and made no comment until I had obviously taken too long and he said "Again". I pushed at him, he absorbed or evaded or whatever it was he was doing to negate my push and each time, I found myself cuffed around the right ear.

I began to feel self-conscious, each time doing the same thing and receiving a cuff around the ear and wondered what the other members of the group must be making of it. I didn't pause, knowing that if I did I would only be commanded to go again. I pushed at him; he cuffed me round the ear.

"Perhaps I don't understand this" I said while pushing him, the only reply being another cuff around the ear. I stopped then and said "Give me something, some idea of what we are doing here."

I thought he would simply tell me to go again, but he mimed the movement his body had been making, showing me how his weight shifted, his centre turned and his arms moved and said "This is called 'playing the lute' by some practitioners." He had frozen in a posture which did resemble someone holding an oversized guitar. He then showed me a formalized way to do the push and asked me to continue.

I pushed; he melted and cuffed me around the ear again. I tried again with a bit more force and this time his left hand cuffing me around the ear almost made me lose my balance entirely and fall.

There was no pain in the light cuffs that Shun Yuan was delivering, no physical pain, but I could feel the frustration rising in me.

Over and over again I pushed and got cuffed around the ear for it until I had to stop again and said, "This seems pointless. I can't remove you from the circle with this push and I'm just getting cuffed around the ear every time I try."

He stood there silently looking at me until I resumed my position and tried again. Once again I got cuffed around the ear. I bit down on my rising frustration and put more effort into it, which only resulted in the ear-cuffing getting more energetic, sometimes knocking me out of my stance and occasionally threatening to knock me to the floor.

A tension had built up in me and I could feel it twisting on my emotions and causing me to get upset. I was feeling like an idiot, but this time not through some mistake I had made on my own part, but because Shun Yuan was treating me like an idiot. I had to show him that I could do it. I had to push him out of that circle and clear out of the practice area so that we could drop this idiotic nonsense and get on with something worthwhile.

My mind flashed back to Master Hong's place and I thought of how he had summoned all his will and strength and focused them through a hammer blow which had destroyed the relic he had held so dear. It was only through such a display of absolute focus that I would be able to show Shun Yuan that I was ready to learn at a new level.

I stood there in front of him, getting my stance exactly as I wanted it to be and readying myself. If he noticed anything different in me he did not betray it and stood utterly motionless, waiting for me to act. When I did move, the forcefulness of my own movement almost took me by surprise. It suddenly burst out of me, a strike more than a push and I heard a voice in my mind saying, "This'll show him."

I sat on the floor where I had landed for a while, holding my ear which was throbbing and ringing in the most alarming fashion. I wasn't sure if he had stricken me deaf with that blow and it took me a while to convince myself that I was still able to hear out of both ears.

I looked up at Shun Yuan then and surprised myself at not feeling angry. In fact I didn't feel anything but stunned. It was as if all the tension and frustration and embarrassment that I had built up inside myself and used to fuel my attack had been knocked clean out of me. The pain and ringing in my ear subsided and I was left feeling strangely clear.

It was a very confusing state to be in and as I looked around I thought the expression on my face must look like a baby's at that moment, full of open wonder at every little thing. As I stood up I suddenly recalled many stories I had read about Buddhist Masters using a well-timed blow to induce a change in their disciple's state of consciousness. I had never really understood those stories until now.
"Is it gone?" I asked Shun Yuan.
"On vacation" he replied. "How do you feel?" he asked "Are you dizzy at all?" I shook my head no and told him that I felt open.
"Again" he said and held out his hand to help me up. I took up my stance and watched as my hand reached out towards his chest incredibly slowly and gently. My hand made contact with him and through it I could feel how his whole body responded. I reached out slightly further testing, but so gently it was as if I was only probing with my mind as opposed to my hand. I felt how each change in the pressure applied through my hand was echoed by a change in his body, which opened up a space into which any force I would apply would dissipate.

I reached further and further, feeling this way and that for anything which would provide an anchor for me to press on, but it felt as if I were pushing against the sheets hanging on my grandmother's washing line.

I could feel exactly how his 'play the lute' method worked, seeing how the motion translated my forward pushing movement into the turning force in his body, which resulted in his left hand coming out and cuffing my ear.

I experimented then, reaching mentally for some way in which I could press my attack without the inevitable result, but could not find one. For a moment then I felt as if we were one single entity, joined as we were through the intensely subtle and tenuous, yet absolutely real channel of his exercise.

Realizing I had shut my eyes I opened them again and looked at Shun Yuan then. He was smiling, that grinning smile of his and where prior to the exercise I had been full of angry frustration towards him, I was now overwhelmed by other emotions of gratitude and happiness and a laugh burst of me and I felt a tear on my cheek.

"It's time to switch" he said, indicating that I should take his place inside the roughly drawn circle.

"It will be back from vacation any second and we need to be ready. This time I will try to push you out and you will play the lute."

I nodded; I could feel my state changing just as he had predicted and by the time I had taken my place I was already telling myself that I had understood his technique and that there was no way he was moving me from this circle.

He stood in front of me and performed the formal pushing movement a few times, allowing me to adjust my position and movement until I felt happy that I had it right.

Then he pushed gently and I stumbled backwards out of the circle. My brow creased as I wondered what I had done wrong and took my place once again. Once again he pushed and try as I might I could not get away from his energy and found myself shoved backwards.

The next time he pushed I forgot all about playing the lute and the desire to cuff him around the ear which had spontaneously risen up from somewhere inside. I focused all my attention on feeling his push and trying to make space as he had done, to allow the energy to dissipate away. I was still in the circle! I hadn't managed any counter-attack, but I had remained on my spot.

He came forward again, slightly more forcefully and I felt myself flinching. His force somehow found that knot of tension and pressed on it, sending me once again out of my circle.

Then he stopped and nodded at me saying "it's back there in full now" and putting his hand ever so gently against my chest.

I closed my eyes and relaxed as I focused every ounce of my attention on the feeling of his palm. I thought I could feel his energy probing at the structure of my stance, even as I had probed out with my mind to test his. I could feel the innermost core of my physical body shifting gently this way and that as it evaded his inquisitive force.

The core of my mental being seemed to be going through a similar exercise. As I shifted physically I also shifted mentally in my desire to avoid further embarrassment, to show that I had learned something and was worth him spending his time with. On and on came the gentle probing force and all the while I shifted this way and that evading him.

I could feel the smile coming over my face as I realized that I had got it and in that very instant he let go a burst of energy that knocked me off my feet and out of the circle, to land on my back with a loud thump. I got up and said "I really thought I had it just then."

"Just before that moment when you thought you had it" he replied, "That's when you had it. But that's exactly when that inner core Rob, we might call it your ego, stepped up to claim ownership of the moment and that's when you lost it. It's always there to take the credit for anything which goes well, but somehow seems to always disappear on vacation when you are facing disaster."

"Then how do you do it?" I asked him.

"The true answer's simple Rob" he replied, "I don't." Seeing that I needed more he went on, "What you are experiencing are some moments when I am out of the way and there is only Tao. You are familiar with the Taoist concept of 'Wu Wei' of doing nothing. Well not being there isn't simply a physical thing Rob; it's not just avoiding or redirecting your force by a particular movement of the body. It has to extend throughout your entire being so that the only true answer I can give you is that I do not do anything at all because I am not present."

I had read about all of these things many times in the course of my studies, but had never come face to face with someone who had taken things beyond the conceptual level and applied them in a real and tangible way.

"Then I guess the thing I have to learn" I said, "is how to not be there. I thought I was getting to that with my meditation sometimes. There have definitely been times when I was simply gone."

"When there is nothing at all to lay claim to" Shun Yuan explained "then that core Rob will also go off on vacation. It's only interested in hanging around when there's something to feed it. The problem is that as soon as you come out of trance and have the feeling that you did a good meditation session, there it is taking the spotlight and claiming the praise. You need to keep finding opportunities to invest in loss and you will gradually feel it more and more clearly when your core Rob disappears. You need to do this in your real life as well as in practice sessions like this. You can start with Morning. Just say sorry and keep your mouth shut. Do it publicly, the more public your humiliation the greater the loss and the more the chance that you will experience your ego running off to hide. Just don't waste the opportunity Rob; you don't get many chances at a real learning like this."

"I think I should go right now" I said. Shun Yuan replied with a nod and asked me to come out to Master Hong's later that evening.

I left the park and started walking home, stopping only to pick up a bottle of water on the way. I had no appetite, not for food nor what I was about to put myself through, but the decision remained firm and I carried on, each step taking me closer to my encounter with Morning's wrath.

When I got back to the tea house I walked in to the staff area to find that Mrs Lim and Sofia were there, sharing breakfast with Morning, Little Rabbit and Swift.

I could only guess at what had been said in my absence, but the five pairs of eyes currently burning holes in my skin led me to think that it had not been good. Morning looked like she was ready to explode. She had taken the art of fuming and raised it to heights that even Shun Yuan's gungfu would struggle to reach.

"I'm so sorry" I said, looking at her and then clamping down hard before there was any chance of blurting out some stupid comment in addition.

The others had stopped eating and sat as if frozen, waiting for Morning's reaction. The silence went on until it was utterly unbearable, each moment that passed feeling like a fresh lash from a whip. Then Morning stood up slowly and walked over to me until she was standing right in front of me, looking up into my face.

"You don't matter" she said and with that she walked out of the room with a little spring in her step.

I stood there reduced to insignificance and watched her go. When I looked back at the table, the others had unfrozen and carried on eating their breakfast, without a word or a glance in my direction.

I turned to go, the feeling of emptiness resulting from Morning's casual dismissal leaving me disoriented and I stumbled as I took a step.

"I'm moving to Kaohsiung to study" said Sofia "so you needn't worry about Friday evening." I mumbled something affirmative in reply and walked out of the staff room and up the stairs to my bedroom.

When I opened the door I saw immediately that the cover on my comforter had been changed for a white one. I sat down and opened my cupboard drawer to get a fresh shirt and found it full of small squares of fabric, yellow and black and white, one of which bore the unmistakable image of the end of Snoopy's nose.

A knock at the door a few minutes later proved to be Mrs Lim, who told me that I was welcome to keep the room, but asked if I would please not drive her girls insane. I promised to do my best and hurriedly changed that into a promise to do better than I had been.

I asked her what we should do about our arrangement, given that Sofia would be going away and she told me that she would think about it and would let me know in due course.

I sat quietly in my room for a long time then. I saw myself standing there in front of Morning, fully expecting an angry castigation which did not come. I couldn't work out which lesson was the harder to take, my realization that I was still jumping from one assumption to the next despite everything I was trying to learn, or the simple fact that I wasn't as important as I thought I was to one young Taiwanese girl.

The lesson did taste very bitter indeed.

Chapter eleven.

The sixth method.

Book learning shimmy.

I was becoming used to feeling dazed and confused a lot of the time, but later that day when Sofia gave me her scooter it threw me for a loop. I had sheepishly asked her if I could borrow it to get across town again and she said I might as well keep hold of the keys as she never used it anyway these days. I'd expected a reprimand, or a continuation of the black looks I had received earlier, but just as Morning had done, Sofia appeared to be putting me out of her mind entirely. She sat in her room reading a mathematics text and when I asked her if she needed any help, she replied "No thanks Rob, don't need any help" without once looking up. Something in me heard this as "I don't need YOUR help" and I left quietly.

    I drove across town to Master Hong's house, eager to see Shun Yuan again. The feeling of empty, open clarity that he had provoked in me previously was something entirely new to me and I felt like I was being drawn inexorably back to my next lesson by possibilities that I had not yet imagined.

    As I drove up to the house I saw that someone was standing in the grassy area beside the house and as I got closer I recognized Wayne.

    He was standing absolutely still, his arms raised in front of his body clearly showing that he was working on a postural exercise. When I got off the scooter and walked over to the house I looked at him closely. His whole body was shaking and he was drenched in sweat. The rate at which this dripped from him alarmed me and I thought he was in real danger of serious dehydration. His face was bright red. In fact every bit of his skin that I could see was bright red.

A loud buzzer rang a single long ring and Wayne reached down to grab a towel to wipe his face and then a large bottle of water which he chugged down in a single go. I could see several other empty bottles strewn around the ground where he stood.

It seemed like only a few seconds had passed when the buzzer rang again, two short bursts in quick succession and Wayne resumed his original standing posture.

I walked over and picked up the empty water bottles, saying that I would refill them for him. I don't know if he even heard me. He had closed his eyes and almost the instant he had taken up his posture his body had started shaking again.

I walked indoors with the bottles and found Shun Yuan and Master Hong in the dining room. Shun Yuan was drawing something in a notebook and he packed this away when I came in.

"From the look of you" he said, "I'd say you've had a lesson. You should find a way to say thanks, but you probably need to do that in such a way that she doesn't know it was you. You will know you've given thanks for something real and that is enough."

I nodded and gestured with my head that I was going to refill the water bottles for Wayne and went into the kitchen to do so. Once I had put the full bottles back where Wayne could get at them I went back into the dining room.

"So what is Wayne doing?" I asked. I had seen many people practicing different variations of these standing exercises which were called "standing post".

"Wayne is eating bitter" replied Master Hong. I turned to Shun Yuan and asked why he hadn't had me doing something similar.

"Yet Rob" he replied with a hint of a smile.

"I haven't had you doing something similar yet. You were quite clear that you wanted to learn how to apply the principles of the Way in your everyday life. Well, given your tendency to compartmentalize everything and separate your practice from your everyday life, it seemed only natural to find a teaching opportunity which arose from a situation that you couldn't possibly isolate from normal day to day living."

"But why is Wayne eating bitter like that?" I asked, peering out through the kitchen as if I could see him through the wall. "Has he come here to study with you?" I was looking at Shun Yuan but Master Hong replied, "Yes, I have accepted Wayne as a student. This is lesson one. Wayne has some remedial work to do before I can begin teaching him Hsing-Yi."

"Is that a test you are putting him through?" I asked. Master Hong sat and thought for a while before answering, "On one level yes, that is a test and Wayne can fail it by deciding to give up and walk off, but he's not just standing there doing some nonsense that I've invented for my own amusement. The posture he is trying to learn will be a foundation for everything else that is to come. Also, he said he needed help getting off the cigarettes. With his mind full of the agony of burning muscles he is not thinking about smoking. Lastly, the bitterness doesn't last forever. If he perseveres his body and mind will undergo changes which will eventually make this a pleasurable exercise and the bitter will become sweet."

At that Master Hong stood up and walked outside to take a look at his new student. I looked across the table at Shun Yuan. He was sitting very still and with his eyes half closed and his hands folded together he reminded me of the large Buddha that I had knelt before in the temple on Baguashan. As I sat watching him I felt a great wave of stillness coming over me, as if he was somehow radiating a quiet peaceful energy which imbued all those it touched with an inner calm. Still watching him I could feel myself gradually getting more and more relaxed.

The scene around me started to take on a curious otherworldly quality which was similar to that which I had experienced after my period of very deep meditation. The colours on the walls started to change, turning from their normal subdued smoky yellow to a much more vibrant yellowish gold.

Shun Yuan himself was reduced to a dark blob and then his hands moved and began tracing curious patterns in the air in front of him which hung ghostly against the black background of his robes, like the after-images on an old television set. His hands, glowing now it seemed, reached out towards me, his extended forefinger touching me on the forehead as he whispered, "Look the other way Rob. It's not out here."

My eyes closed then and I had the sensation of falling backwards into myself. As I fell, I could feel the icy cold spot where his finger had touched me and as I looked at this spot I saw a dot of light, which expanded until I was suddenly watching a scene being played out behind my closed eyes, as clear as if I was watching it on the screen in a darkened cinema. The moment I tried to hold on to the image to understand what was happening in the scene though, it changed. The changes began happening quicker and quicker until every image that arose immediately changed into something else the moment my awareness caught it.

I sat there for a while and watched the raw torrent of

images that my mind was generating until Shun Yuan tapped me on the forehead again and said "That's enough for now I think."

"What was that?" I asked, blinking my eyes as I let them adjust. "All those images, I've never experienced anything like that."

"I would say you've never paid attention to anything like that" he replied. "That was your mind talking, part of it anyway."

"It was all jumbled and confused" I said. "It kept changing so fast that I couldn't keep up and had to just sort of watch it flowing by without trying to hold on to it."

"It looked jumbled and confused because you haven't learned the language that this part of your mind is speaking in, but that will come with time. Sometimes you'll find it flowing by at incredible speed, other times it might slow right down or even seem to stop."

"How am I going to learn how to understand it?" I asked.

"You can try saying what you are seeing into a tape recorder and listening to it later" he said, adding "Don't worry if you can't catch everything. You don't need to try and catch every image and every transformation as it happens. Just record what you can and you will gradually come to an understanding of the language that these images are being presented to you in. Over time as your ability to focus improves, you will find that you can follow more and more clearly and feel like you are missing less and less. If you have real difficulty with this let me know and I'll give you something else to help you. I think you can start your meditation sessions again, but from now on when you are meditating, observe this river of images and make a recording for yourself. You will be very surprised at what you start learning."

"It feels like the Bagua" I said, recalling how the form I had seen Shun Yuan demonstrating looked like a continuous flow of energy, transforming the body from one shape to the next as the performer went round and round the circle.

Shun Yuan smiled a little smile at that and nodded saying, "These practices exist on many levels and this is perhaps the most purely mental level that I have come across. The effort here is very different though. The deep creative part of your mind that generates all this is inexhaustible and does so effortlessly, but the conscious awareness part of you that is trying to follow along and record what you are seeing will get a real workout. The ancient Greeks called this method 'Wrestling with the God Proteus'." I made a mental note to myself to go and get a Greek mythology book as soon as I could.

Shun Yuan stood then and led me out to the grassy area, where Wayne was still working. His body seemed to be shaking less. Master Hong walked around him making adjustments to his posture, most of which were so subtle that I couldn't tell what had changed. Shun Yuan asked me to perform my circling and I struggled to recall what he had shown me before.

The expression on his face looked like he was wincing in pain and I stopped then and said "I know it's terrible. I have real difficulty with my balance and with keeping on the circle."

He was shaking his head then and said, "None of that matters at this point Rob. What matters is why you knew I was not happy with your effort. Can you tell me that?"

"From the look on your face" I answered. He looked at me then, with that same look that I had grown to recognize and I knew that he was expecting me to come up with something more.

I took up the posture again, extending my hand to the

centre and walked around a few more circuits, glancing over at him for any cue however small.

"I don't think the posture is that bad" I said, "But I can't seem to help wandering off the circle all the time."

"Rob, you will never make a good circle like this. Your attention is all over the place. That's how you knew I was making a face, because you were looking at me when you should have been concentrating here." With that he grabbed the tip of the forefinger of my extended arm and went on, "Intent Rob, focused intent. You need to work on becoming absolutely focused towards the centre of the circle. The physical posture is much less important for your needs at this stage. The same focus that you develop here, while walking the circle, is the same focus that will enable you to follow the river of imagery that your mind offers to you. The strength you are building now is the same strength that you will use to wrestle Proteus, understand?"

It clicked and I nodded and got ready to start up again, but Shun Yuan held up his hand for me to wait and walked off around the back of the house. He returned a minute later with a long bamboo cane his hand.

"Training wheels" he said, planting the beanpole in the middle of the area where I was circling and tying a white ribbon to it at the same level as my eyes.

"There, that should help" and with that he nodded to me to carry on. I focused my gaze and fixed my attention on the centre of the circle, trusting to my peripheral vision to keep me aware of what was happening around me. I started to walk around and almost immediately I had the feeling that the whole world was spinning around the outside of my circle. I very quickly became dizzy and a stumble brought me to a stop.

"I couldn't keep going teacher," I apologized, but Shun Yuan was looking at me with a big smile on his face.

"You only get dizzy that quickly when you are really focusing properly Rob! It's a good sign." Once more I had to adjust my notions of success and failure and went back to try again. Once more I became very quickly dizzy.

"Turn the circle a bit more slowly" he said, "Perhaps two thirds of the speed you are going now."

I slowed down a bit and found that I was able to walk around for quite a while longer before the dizziness returned.

"Keep going like that" said Shun Yuan, turning away to go and speak to Master Hong. I carried on walking, stopping momentarily each time the dizziness became too much for me. I lost track of time and of how many times I had walked around the circle. I became very conscious of each step, particularly when my foot landed poorly on a rough patch of ground and caused me to wobble violently and almost fall over.

After what could have been hours, Shun Yuan came back to me and had me stop and step back from my practice area. I was very satisfied to see the beginnings of a circle being worn on the ground where I had been walking.

Shun Yuan showed me how to change the focus of my gaze and instructed me to do this before I had become so dizzy that I couldn't carry on. He then asked me to give it a try. The technique was remarkably simple and I spent some time then walking around my circle and controlling my dizziness with the changing focus of my eyes, much in the same way as I imagined a ballet dancer or whirling dervish must control theirs by focusing momentarily on a distant fixed spot.

Shun Yuan called out to me to stop and nodded approval at my efforts.

"Remember Rob, focused intent. That intent will form a channel and your energy will arise and flow along that channel and then..." he stopped himself and concluded, "Well let's not get too far ahead of ourselves. That's good work for tonight Rob. Meet me in the park at five again." Something came over me and I bowed deeply in thanks to Shun Yuan for the lessons and said "I am so happy that you have taken me beyond my book learning. I think I might have been stuck forever as an armchair Adept if I hadn't met you."

"It's late Rob" he replied simply. I looked at my watch. It was after midnight and I realized that I hadn't eaten anything all day, but weirdly did not feel at all hungry. I jumped on the scooter and went home to frantically scribble everything I could remember in my journal.

I found a letter from Mrs Lim lying on my comforter when I got to my room. She was proposing that I do some translation work for her brother's business and had left an example of the kind of thing they needed doing and an offer of a small wage along with the room and board I was getting. I sat there and remembered the sense of bonding I had had with her and her family and felt it coming back even stronger. I had no idea why this woman was helping me in this way and felt like a lost orphan who had been rescued by a kind benefactor.

I didn't see Mrs Lim in the morning, so hastily wrote an acceptance note, hoping that she would understand my hurriedly scrawled handwriting. My handwritten Chinese was not good at the best of times, suffering from a lack of practice and overreliance on the keyboard. I pushed the note under her door and made my way to the park.

When I arrived I saw Shun Yuan there practising with Peng. English Paul was there again and I spent some time watching him perform his Taiji routine. Paul had clearly benefited from his chats with Mr Tsai and I looked on with admiration at the power and grace which he exuded, giving a little clap and a nod in his direction when had finished.

I turned my attention back to Shun Yuan and Peng, who were working with the 'Play the lute' motion together but going back and forth, each one in turn gently pushing and then defending from the push.

I jumped a little as a tap on my shoulder came with a soft voice saying, "Hello Rob". I looked around to see Gareth smiling at me.

"How do you do that?" I asked.

"Were you a ninja in a past life or something? How does someone as big as you move about so quietly?" He just grinned in response and asked how things were going, telling me that he was on his way out of the country for a short trip.

I told him that I was studying with Shun Yuan and he said, "I wanted to speak to him today, I'm glad he's here" and giving a small bow as he entered the practice area, he walked over to where Shun Yuan and Peng were now standing in discussion.

"I've come back for more!" Gareth announced as he shook hands with each man in turn.

"I think I've learned something important from the last time and I would really like the chance to test out my understanding if you don't mind."

Shun Yuan nodded and he and Gareth walked over to a clear space in the practice area. Gareth had an odd look on his face, a secret smile almost as he went through some limbering up movements. Shun Yuan stood there watching him with the same air of open attentiveness that I had frequently observed in him. Gareth finished his stretching and asked if Shun Yuan were ready to proceed and Shun Yuan nodded in reply.

Gareth took up a huge posture. To me he looked like a sumo wrestler, with legs deep in a strong stance and arms wide open to either side. Shun Yuan twisted on the spot so that he had one side facing Gareth, his head seemed to be tucked slightly down.

Gareth erupted out of his stance with a roar and I could not believe how quickly he crossed the gap between them and engaged Shun Yuan. His huge arms came together like the pincers of a gigantic crab and as I looked on I was stunned to see that he had captured Shun Yuan in a headlock.

I felt my pulse hammering as I looked on. This wasn't how David and Goliath was supposed to go! I wasn't ready to watch my teacher get defeated in front of me, let alone squeezed to a pulp.

Shun Yuan's body shook violently and his left foot stamped hard on the ground, causing his left knee to strike Gareth in the back of the right leg. This time the gentle giant was toppled all the way to the ground, letting out an ear-splitting cry as he fell. His arms flew away from Shun Yuan's neck as he grabbed at his own lower leg. The next moment he had mastered himself and sat there shaking his head and rubbing his calf.

Shun Yuan helped him up and Gareth hobbled over to sit on one of the stone benches while Peng fetched some ointment, which he handed to the big man.

"I should've known" said Gareth, wincing as he rubbed the ointment into his leg.

"The last time my strength was focused so tightly it was easy to avoid, this time I've expanded it way out and you've popped it like a balloon! I still have some work to do."

The two of them shook hands and Shun Yuan turned and looked at me and said "Queen to B8, check!" I kicked myself again for not having paid more attention during that first meeting and resolved to have him take me through the chess game from beginning to end at the very next opportunity.

I spent the rest of the session that morning sitting on the bench and watching as the others went through their various exercises. Once Gareth had recovered he performed a number of routines and I was again left amazed at how someone so big could move so nimbly.

When they were all done, six of us decided to go to Peng's favourite breakfast place together. We walked along in pairs; Gareth chatting with English Paul, Peng walking with Mr Tsai and chatting away in Taiwanese and Shun Yuan and I brought up the rear.

Peng announced that he was treating everybody that day and insisted that we order a huge variety of dishes. I thought that we had probably bought everything on the menu and thanked Peng as I enjoyed my breakfast.
"How did you do that just now?" I asked Shun Yuan, wanting to kick myself as soon as the question had come out of my mouth, but to my surprise he answered.
"You aren't going to like it if I tell you. I don't think you'll believe me and that will damage our relationship Rob."
"Go on" I insisted, "I really want to hear it. I understand conceptually what you two were talking about, how his energy was all spread out and how you managed to pop it. I'm just wondering about the specific movement you used."
"I saw it in that book you've been carrying around" he said, gesturing towards my bag with his chopsticks.

I looked at him hard then, searching for any sign that he was joking and then sighed and thought I would just have to believe him and if I was laughed at because of my naivety then so be it. I reached into the bag and pulled out the book. It was a book from my collection of reprints of old Chinese martial arts texts and I had completely forgotten it was there. I handed it to him.

"Show me" I said and he flipped through the pages until he found what he was looking for.

"There" he said, pointing at the page. I looked, fully expecting to hear him break out in laughter at having fooled me but there it was, a sequence of drawings and some text explaining a low kicking technique used as a response to a head-lock.

"Don't be too quick to dismiss the book learning completely Rob. Who knows, if I hadn't seen that the other day, we might be sitting in the hospital now and Gareth here might be explaining to his Master why he had squeezed me half to death." A quick translation and explanation later and there was laughter, which the whole group shared and I sat there in the company of my teacher and my training friends and felt deeply happy.

Later that day Mrs Lim and I shook hands on our new agreement and she introduced me to her brother. We sat together in the tea house going through the work he needed doing and we arranged that he would drop off the work to me in batches and collect the finished pieces the following week. He also mentioned that his company was having a big dinner and asked if I would like to come. I said I'd be delighted and asked if I could bring some friends along, intending to invite Shun Yuan and Peng and perhaps one or two of the other folks from the park. Mr Lim was happy to oblige, telling me the more the merrier and that he would let me know when the final date and location for the dinner had been settled.

I felt glad that I could give some small gift to the group. It had struck me that Shun Yuan had never asked for anything from me in return for his teaching.

Chapter twelve.

The seventh method.

Dog boxing? Or did you just levitate?

Over the next few weeks my life settled into another new rhythm. I got up shortly before five in the morning to go down to the park and practise with Shun Yuan, Peng and the rest of the group.

I spent the early part of the day working on whatever study assignments I had been set and then set to work on Mr Lim's translations. The work was challenging and varied and although it was all in one direction, from Chinese to English, my Chinese vocabulary and understanding of the use of the language in different contexts was hugely improved and at one stage I found myself limited more by my English language abilities.

In the late afternoon or early evening, when I had finished the work I had assigned to myself to complete for the day, I rode over to Master Hong's house.

Wayne was there all the time now and I learned that he had moved in with Master Hong. He worked with a variety of postures now, still holding them for long periods of time and had completely transformed from the shaking sweaty wreck that I had encountered that evening some weeks back. When he took up a posture his energy and the strength of his intent was so powerful it felt to me as if as if he were carved in granite.

I thought back to my first impressions of the man, rudely barging in to the practice area and then standing there blowing his cigarette smoke at us and throwing his butt to the floor. I had to admit that this was no longer the same person. Wayne had clearly made his mind up to make a change and the results were already showing.

Shun Yuan began helping me to refine my circling technique, showing me ways of sensing where I was on the circle with my peripheral vision by dividing the circle up, first into what he called primary quadrants and then into a pie with eight pieces.

The difficulty of the circling increased exponentially when he had me walk around with my legs bent quite a fair amount at the knee. In this posture, even when circling quite slowly I found myself getting exhausted very quickly. Shun Yuan's advice was always the same, to persevere but not to push too hard against the signals that my body was sending me. If I learned to listen to my body he said, there would come a time when it would listen to me.

I found myself thinking of some of the incidents I had observed while with him, how he had always somehow managed at the very last possible instant to transform the situation and come out on top.

At one point Shun Yuan removed the beanpole which had acted as my training wheels and to the expression on my face he replied by asking me, "What are training wheels for Rob?"

"They stop you falling off and smashing your head on the ground?" I tried.

"It's more subtle than that" he replied.

"They give you the confidence that you won't fall off and smash your head on the ground and that allows you to relax. Try to remember when you learned to ride your bike, or to swim. Being able to relax was an essential part of finding your balance or of knowing that you could float. Once you've relaxed, leaving the training wheels on risks turning them into a crutch and preventing you from progressing any further."

I had indeed relaxed a lot into my circle walking and found that removing the beanpole actually improved my circling, forcing me as it did to develop the subtle balance of awareness required; my directed attention highly focused towards the centre of the circle, while my more diffuse peripheral awareness was taking in information from all around me.

On more than one occasion this bifurcation of my awareness created a distinctly altered state in me and each time I was surprised again to find the time had flown by.

During resting periods I spent a lot of time watching Master Hong perform his Hsing-Yi. The two arts could not have been more different, but I could see the way in which they complemented one another and I could understand when Master Hong told me that they were taught together in many schools.

Master Hong also decided that I should learn to cook and I spent many evenings in his kitchen, struggling to lift the massive wok in which our food was prepared. He had enormously strong hands and wrists and always laughed at my clumsy double-handed attempts to lift the wok full of food by the handle and then to shake the food gingerly into the bowl for serving.

Before each meal, Master Hong liked to recite a mantra, which he did in a deep monotone chant. One evening I was surprised to hear Wayne joining in, his higher tone managing a very satisfying harmony with that of his Master. I couldn't understand the words that they were reciting and when I asked Master Hong about this, he told me that the words were originally Sanskrit. He said that he spoke a silent prayer to apologize for his terrible pronunciation before he began the mantra, which he said was an invocation of the characteristics of the various deities which he revered. He looked over at Shun Yuan then and asked him to give a rendition of the Great Compassion Dharani. "Bring me the bowl and the fish then" said Shun Yuan and Master Hong sent Wayne off to bring them while I sat there, my brow creasing as I cast a confused look about me.

Wayne came back with his hands full. In one hand he was carrying a bowl made of hammered metal which I recognized as the bowl Shun Yuan had had with him that first day at the tea house. In the other hand he carried a round wooden object and when I saw it I understood what Shun Yuan had meant by "fish".

The wooden fish is a percussion instrument which is used to keep time when reciting chants, the round hollow shape making a very distinctive sound when it is struck. These instruments are commonly carved with patterns resembling fish scales and may have eyes carved on them also. The un-lidded, unblinking fish eye representing eternal vigilance. This example was highly ornate and really resembled a fat goldfish.

Shun Yuan pulled at his robe and a length of cloth came away from where it had been tucked. He folded this and placed it on the table and then took the items from Wayne and placed them on the cloth.

In his left hand he held the wooden striker which was paired with his metal bowl and in his right hand he held another striker, with which he would strike the wooden fish. He started singing the Dharani and I immediately recognized the tune, which I had heard so often playing softly at the tea house.

With each beat, he struck the wooden fish which made a

deeply satisfying "bok, bok, bok" and seemed to punctuate the words he was singing. On occasion, at moments that seemed completely random to me, he also struck the metal bowl gently and this rang with its own sharp metallic tone that was in distinct contrast to the soft hollow sound of the wooden fish.

As the singing went on I closed my eyes and allowed myself to drift and enjoy the feelings that the Dharani brought up in me. After some time the singing stopped and that Master Hong and Wayne had also really enjoyed the experience and seemed to be returning from whatever deep reverie the rendition had taken them on.

Shun Yuan sat there quietly for a while and then put the wooden fish and it's striker to one side and placed the metal bowl directly in front of him. Then he took the wooden striker and used this to stroke the bowl around the outside of its rim. The bowl started to hum, the sound getting stronger and richer until it was producing a fabulous deep tone. This pulsed, now louder now softer, to some hidden rhythm and was entirely unlike the harsh tone which was made when the bowl was struck.

Shun Yuan stopped then and took a breath. With his left hand on his chest and his right hand pointing up at the ceiling he let out a single tone, drawing it out longer and longer, sending shivers down my spine and giving me goose-bumps all over my body. He gave no explanation and I did not request one, but just sat quietly enjoying the peacefulness of the moment.

Our evening sessions always ended late, frequently going on to midnight or later and I was really surprised that I was able to continue functioning on so little sleep. I did not manage a meditation session every evening, but when I did I spent the time recording the flow of images into my tape recorder which only seemed to intensify the experience. It felt strange, but I soon got used to the double awareness required to observe the flow of images and record it without disrupting it. I found myself reflecting on Shun Yuan's comment that the focus I developed while circling would also be beneficial for this meditative work and began getting a deeper feeling for how the physical and mental practices were interconnected.

"What do you do for money?" I asked Shun Yuan one evening. I recalled that I had never actually seen anyone ask him to pay for anything, but there must have been occasions where he needed cash.
"That really depends where I am Rob" he replied.
"It is permitted for me to carry money while travelling, but at the moment for instance I am being looked after by my dear friend Master Hong."

I walked back into the house and found Master Hong peeling sweet potatoes while watching something on the television. He gestured towards the screen and announced, "Eight Steps of the Heavenly Dragon. Do you know it? It's a great series."

I turned to look at the screen and as I watched for a minute or two my mind struggled with the experience. I was in the house of a Master of gungfu and here he was, peeling vegetables and watching a martial arts soap opera on the TV.
"May I disturb you for a moment with a question?" I asked.
"Yes, of course" he replied, not taking his eyes off the screen as he threw one peeled sweet potato into a bucket and reached out for another.
"Why do you host Shun Yuan?" I asked; adding, "If it's not too impolite to ask."
"I think it's a natural enough question" he replied, "and I don't consider you impolite to ask it, but it's simply too

personal a matter to go into. I have known Shun Yuan for a long time now so let's just say that I look after him because he is my friend."

"Should I be paying him for my lessons?" I asked.

"I mean I'm not sure how he survives."

"Has he asked you to?" Master Hong enquired, to which I shook my head and he carried on saying, "Then I would say this situation is a lesson which he is offering you. You should reflect on your question and come to a decision."

I left Master Hong then and really got to wondering about Shun Yuan's life. I had expected, or at least hoped for, simple answers to my questions and I really had expected that Master Hong would reply yes, I should pay Shun Yuan for my lessons. Or was it no? Would he be offended if I offered him money? I decided to ask Mrs Lim for advice. I thought that it was about time that I sought out her wisdom where Shun Yuan was concerned.

I approached her one lunchtime and told her that I had been spending more and more time with Shun Yuan and thanked her for that day, when she had been the catalyst for our first getting together. She gave me a nod and a smile at that, with a look that said she knew exactly what she was doing when she had directed me to go and intrude on the privacy of a total stranger.

I remembered what Shun Yuan had said that day, about how Mrs Lim took care of him because she liked the way that he recited the Great Compassion Dharani and when I told her this she burst out laughing.

"I do love his rendition" she told me, "but no, that's not it at all."

She showed me to the tiny household shrine which stood under the stairs and took a small box down from its place, giving a little bow as she did so. This was nothing like the shrine in Master Hong's house, being only a simple shelf with a small Buddha statuette, a single incense stick burning in a holder and one or two other trinkets.

"Shun Yuan was first here years ago, before he joined the Order, while my husband was still alive. He met my husband through a mutual acquaintance and came here for dinner one day. They got to talking about religion and my husband decided to show him this, it's a relic from the ashes of an old Master."

I nodded, excited that I would finally get a chance to see one of these relics up close. Mrs Lim opened the box and handing it to me I saw the relic; a small roundish blob nestling in a bed of red leaves.

It was mostly off-white but had yellowish-brown and green concentric rings running across it and a darker splodge in the centre of these.

I choked down the desire to ask Mrs Lim if Shun Yuan had challenged her late husband to smash the relic to bits and as I held the little box and turned it this way and that I got the eerie impression that it looked like a miniature eyeball staring out at me.

Mrs Lim reached up and took down another box which she opened, this one containing another relic, much smaller, which was ivory white.

"The one you are holding was white like this one" she said. "It had always been white. But that evening when my husband opened the box to show it to Shun Yuan he almost collapsed to see the change in colour. My husband was convinced Shun Yuan was a magical being from that moment on. You've seen his eyes."

I wasn't sure what to make of this at all and just stood there for a while looking at the relic with its coloured bands and pupil-like splodge. I could easily bring Shun Yuan's face to mind, but had never paid any attention to the colour of his eyes and could only curse myself at my lack of awareness.

Mrs Lim carried on, "My husband was a bit afraid of him for a while then, but over time they became very good friends. In fact Shun Yuan worked for months with my husband when the roof of this place started leaking terribly and we didn't have enough money to fix it and replace all the tatamis that were ruined."

I handed the little box back to Mrs Lim and tried to juggle the various pieces of her story in my mind. I had no doubt that she was being sincere, but I struggled deeply with the idea that the relic had changed colour, as much as I struggled with the notion that the late Mr Lim, a modern day man, had a belief system that allowed him to think that a young stranger was a magical being.

Mrs Lim saw me attempting to work through all this and said, "There are many strange phenomena and beliefs that are entwined with our daily lives Rob. You only have to scratch the surface of modern day Taiwan to discover you have been carried back to a much older time indeed." I nodded in agreement at that and told myself that I would take a good look at Shun Yuan's eyes the next time I saw him.

"Do you think Shun Yuan would be offended if I were to pay him some money for the lessons he is teaching me?" I asked.

"Shun Yuan isn't a person to easily take offence" replied Mrs Lim, which answered my question but left me none the wiser as to how I should actually act.

In the end I made a spur of the moment decision and put some money in a red envelope, intending to hand this formally to Shun Yuan the next morning. Although red envelopes are more typically used when giving gifts of money at New Year or at weddings, I felt that the event of becoming his student was significant enough to warrant the use.

Once again he was already there when I arrived at the park and as I walked towards him I felt incredibly nervous. My emotions seemed to have become amplified since meeting him and this was especially the case when I was in his physical presence.

He was standing talking to someone that I didn't know personally but recognized as another teacher who regularly held classes in the park, so as I approached the last few feet I called out to him.

"Good morning teacher, I have something for you." I opened my bag and took out the red envelope and did my best at handing this over in a formal manner. Shun Yuan took the envelope with a small bow of his head and it disappeared into his black robe.

As I looked him in the eye I saw the green and yellow colouration and smiled to myself and bowed back. I did find the things that he did magical, in the same way as I had found the skills of the Li brothers magical and suddenly the late Mr Lim's belief system did not feel so alien or remote to me at all.

I spent that morning circling and Shun Yuan continually spoke to me as I went round, telling me how I should adjust my posture. Occasionally he had me stop and demonstrated while I watched, taking great care over the shape that my upper body, arms and hands should hold while I walked.

He spent a particularly long time ensuring that I was making the right shape with my hands, telling me that the whole body was represented in the hands and that their position could be used to great effect to balance one's energies.

"Like a mudra" I said, and he gave me his smile and a nod in reply.

My body felt like it was doing two exercises at once; the upper body holding a fixed posture in very much the same way as I had seen Wayne doing, while my legs walked continually around and around the circle in the bent kneed fashion which he had shown me and which made the walking so much harder.

The adjustments Shun Yuan was making to my posture and to the position of my arms and hands seemed tiny on the surface and I bet that a casual observer would have been hard pressed to see anything at all, but as the minutes became hours the difference they made became gradually more and more obvious to me internally.

I was fascinated by the feeling that my body was learning an entirely new language of movement and every correction he made awoke my muscles to a new serving of bitterness. Again and again I found myself clenching my teeth and had to remind myself to relax into the exercise and to listen to my body when it needed a break. This was very difficult to do when all I wanted was to show my teacher that I was working hard and getting better at what he was showing me. More than once he had to call out to me to stop and relax for a few moments when my tension had built up so much that it became externally obvious.

We were almost ready to wrap up for the morning when a young man approached. I thought his soft features made him look no older than a child, but had still never been successful in guessing the ages of any of my Chinese acquaintances, blessed as they were with universally youthful looks.

His hair was cropped very short, which made me think he might be a student at a military or police academy and he was dressed in a blue and white tracksuit which bore a logo of a fist and some writing in what I thought I recognized as being Korean. He carried a matching bag, into which he stuffed various personal items as he walked towards us.

If he introduced himself I did not catch it, but pointing over to the other side of the park he said that he had been directed to Shun Yuan by a friend. The young man asked Shun Yuan if he would help him with his sweeping leg technique, as he wished to enter a competition in the weeks ahead and wanted to make sure that his sweep was good enough. He said that none of his fellow students and not even his teacher could withstand the technique, but that in competition with a stranger he might find it more difficult to pull it off. His friend had told him that there was a foreigner in the park who regularly welcomed others to practise with him and said that perhaps he would be willing to let him test out his technique. Although he felt awkward asking, he would very much like the chance to do so.

Shun Yuan nodded in the same casual way I had seen him do before, asking the young man to go ahead when he was ready and I quickly backed away a couple of steps. I had seen many different leg sweeping techniques done by different people in the park, but they all shared the key purpose which was to knock the opponent's legs from under them and sweep them to the floor.

I was thinking that this would be a hard task as I remembered how solidly Shun Yuan seemed connected to the ground, when the young man quickly stepped in close, grabbed Shun Yuan by the shoulders and threw him over his hip. This was nothing like any leg sweeping technique I had ever seen, bearing a much greater resemblance to a judo throw.

Whatever the case, it had taken Shun Yuan completely

off guard and I watched as his head began to fly backwards. It's difficult to describe what happened next. Shun Yuan's body appeared to hang there in the air and pivot around his lower abdomen which was fixed in place. Even as his head and shoulders were being thrust towards the floor, his feet flew up behind the young man's head and grappled him around the neck. Then they were both falling together and Shun Yuan's body twisted as they fell so that when they landed, he was half sitting on the youngster's chest.

I stood there stunned for a while and the young man begged Shun Yuan to teach him the move. Shun Yuan shook his head, trying over and over to explain that he could not teach the youngster how to perform the technique. He obviously thought that Shun Yuan was deliberately denying him and continued to beg for the secret, until eventually Shun Yuan told him that he should find a Master of Dog Boxing, a form which contained very similar methods. He apologized that he did not however know of any Master personally to whom he could make an introduction.

The young man eventually left with a look of deep disappointment on his face and as he went I looked at Shun Yuan and said, "Dog boxing? Or did you levitate just then?" I surprised myself with my own seriousness in asking the question.

"Oh come on Rob, get real" he replied and wandered off to speak to Peng. I stood there looking at my teacher and realizing that his Way had brought him out on top again, this time literally.

Chapter thirteen.

The eighth method.

The eye of the storm.

I wasn't even sure where the idea had come from when I asked Mrs Lim if she knew someone that could teach me how to chant the Great Compassion Dharani. I think I was thinking of surprising Shun Yuan with a recital. The smile that Mrs Lim gave me in response was nothing short of beautiful and she gave me a CD and a little book which had the words written in Chinese, along with phonetic symbols to give the correct pronunciation. I was familiar with these already as they were the same symbols used by children when they began learning to read. They had been introduced to me when I first began learning Chinese and I was happy to find that I could easily follow along at the pace of the CD.

As I repeated the words, trying to commit them to memory, I thought to myself that this was unlike any sing-along CD I had ever heard of. The new flavour given to this incredibly common occurrence struck me as very odd for a moment and caused me to stop. Then I realized that I loved this oddness and carried on.

My dream had started to recur. Almost every night now I found myself walking along the path over the hill and down to the sand with Shun Yuan, except instead of walking up the beach he had now taken to running out into the water, whereupon a huge swell would come up and I would watch from the shore as he surfed through a perfect tunnel caused by the breaking over of the wave. Each night he would beckon to me to come into the water and every time I tried to do so I woke up as soon as my foot got wet.

I hadn't experienced recurring dreams before and asked Shun Yuan if he could give me any advice about them. He told me of a peculiar practice carried out by some Orders, where new novices were initiated in their dreams, after being taught how to seed the dream and then how to become conscious while they were dreaming. He also had me meticulously record my dreams whenever I could recall them and I found that the intention to remember and record my dreams meant that I did in fact remember them more frequently and in greater detail.

This made me think of the observation of breath exercises I had been doing and how the rhythm of my heartbeat changed as I tried to use it as a timer for my breathing. I had the distinct impression that every part of me was malleable and that Shun Yuan was teaching me how to use my focused intent to shape myself.

One night the dream took a very strange turn. We started as usual, walking along the path together, over the hill and down to the sand. Then I turned towards the sea but Shun Yuan was not there and I found myself alone on the stretch of beach. I started walking along the beach and after a while I saw the group of young men coming towards me. I stopped and watched as they approached. The leader of the group stepped forward then, reaching into his pocket as he did so, then suddenly lashed out and slit my throat. The gagging choking agony was absolutely real and I fell to my knees clutching at my throat as my life spilt away into the sand and my cry of anguish was a sickening gurgle.

I came awake slowly that morning and lying there very still I thought to myself "I've survived it!" absolutely convinced that the episode had been real. My eyes still closed, I thought that I must be in the hospital and my hand reached ever so slowly and gently towards my throat to feel the dressing on my wound. When my hand touched my bare throat my eyes came open and I lay there confused for a while before realizing where I was and that the whole thing had been a dream.

As I was getting on the scooter to ride back to the tea house after our session one evening, Shun Yuan replied to my "See you in the park" saying that he would not be able to come to the park in the mornings for a while, as he had something else to attend to at the same time. Although I thought I would start making mistakes without his oversight, he told me that this was simply the training wheels lesson repeated and that I needed to be able to work on my own in confidence.

Strangely enough, I seemed to hear his voice correcting me each morning that I worked in the park without him. I had heard his comments so many times that my mind now repeated them automatically to me every time I caught myself drifting off my circle or slouching out of posture. I was certain that he had invented some excuse to be away from the park in the mornings and wondered briefly if I should turn up unannounced at Master Hong's house one morning to see if he was there.

My circling was definitely improving and I was now walking a strict eight steps around each rotation, my feet landing in almost the exact same spot every time around. My attention focused towards the centre of the circle had become very strong and my peripheral awareness feeding me with the blurred image of the world spinning around outside my circle had ceased making me dizzy. I almost never wandered off the circle now and my speed had gradually picked up until I was now walking with bent knees at least as quickly as I had been doing in the easier more straight-legged walking gait.

My upper body posture had improved also, so that Shun Yuan had stopped having to give a continual running commentary to correct me each evening, but only made mention of a point now and again.

One afternoon I arrived at Master Hong's house to find that my circle had had eight paving slabs arranged on it and Shun Yuan told me to step from one slab to the next.

I could not understand why this was as difficult as it proved to be. The paving slabs were only a couple of inches thick and much of that had sunk into the ground so they were only raised up a fraction, yet walking around on them I felt like I was walking between footholds that were precariously balanced on the tops of ten-foot poles.

It was incredibly difficult to keep my attention focused on the centre of the circle and step around the slabs without continually looking down to check where my feet were landing.

After a while, Shun Yuan arranged another circle of slabs inside this first one and on this tighter inner circle I was able to make smaller steps, go more slowly and feel my way around. Slowing down made me infinitely more aware of what was going on in my body and gave me a far greater degree of control.

When I mentioned this to Shun Yuan he showed me a posture called "Wu Ji" which one might translate as "nothingness" and left me to stand in this posture, telling me to come in when I had learned something and could share it with the others.

I found the posture very relaxing and as I stood there, with my eyes closed and my breathing and heartbeat slowing down, I experienced the same stillness that came over me during meditation. I did not have a tape recorder with me and had not been given any instructions to also watch the images that my mind generated, so simply allowed myself to be absorbed by the stillness.

Some time passed and I went into the house where Wayne was sitting at dinner with Shun Yuan and Master Hong. I was not invited to sit down, so I stood there at the doorway while I described the profound stillness which had come over me.

At this Shun Yuan looked at Wayne and said, "Tell him Wayne." In response, while slurping up a huge mouthful of noodles, Wayne jabbed his chopsticks in the direction of the shrine. Seeing me looking vacantly he said, "Read that, over there" indicating a piece of calligraphy which hung just to the side of the shrine. I read the Characters and stood there absorbing their meaning.

"If in the centre of your stillness there is no movement, this is not gungfu".

I turned around and walked back out to the grass and stood again in the Wu Ji posture, but I was unable to relax due to my growling stomach. The smell of Master Hong's cooking had captured me and try as might, the only thing I could think about was noodles. I went back inside and said, "I have to eat something. I can't do anything but think about food now." Shun Yuan nodded at that and invited me to sit and eat.

"When did you learn to read Chinese?" I asked Wayne, astonished at another new aspect of his transformation.

"I've started learning Chinese from Master" he said, "but they told me what that said just before you walked in." I looked at Shun Yuan and Master Hong, who were grinning around mouthfuls of noodles.

My circling practice began to draw attention in the park and I regularly had strangers approach me to ask what I was studying. They were always surprised to hear that it was Bagua and always shocked to hear that I was learning with a foreigner.

I wasn't sure what to think when one morning Old Li came over and stood watching me intently as I circled, then walked off without saying a word. The next day he was back with several other folk and I felt an intense sense of pride when he told them that this was how to build real gungfu. I wished again and again that Shun Yuan was there to claim his glory, even as I realized that that was entirely unlike him.

I went over to Old Li's spot in the park the following day to thank him and let him know that I valued his opinion enormously. He gave me a sad look then and again stated his worry that the arts would die out.
"The young generation just won't spend time doing the basics like that" he said "they want everything today, to see immediate results for their efforts." Then nodding in Honey's direction he said, "I am very lucky to have a student like her. She will soon have learned everything that I have to give her and then will just need to mature her art."

I looked at her as she performed her routine and wondered if I had it within me to get to anywhere close to her level.

A few days later the dream changed again. I walked over the hill with Shun Yuan and again, by the time I had reached the sand I was alone. I looked out at the sea which was perfectly calm and saw it as a shimmering electric blue, the white flashes which ran in zigzags all across the surface looking like tiny lightning bolts. A majestic white horse ran across the surface of the sea towards me, its hooves making a hissing buzzing noise as they struck the lightning bolts. It stopped right at the water's edge while I patted its nose, then turned and galloped off, disappearing over the horizon. I reached down and filled my cup with water and took a long drink. The water was icy cold and as it hit my stomach I looked down at myself to see my entire body glowing bright blue, except my heart which was an intense ruby red in my chest. I realized that I was dreaming and for a moment savoured the incredible energy running through me. Then I began to get overwhelmed by the strength of the sensations and decided that I needed to wake up, but I could not work out how to do so. I shouted to myself "out, out, out!" and somehow forced myself to sit upright and I came awake, my whole body trembling with energy and all my hair standing on end.

Then the day of Mr Lim's company dinner arrived. He had had unexpected difficulty with booking a suitable location and in the end, with the very short notice I was able to give, only Shun Yuan, Peng and Master Hong were able to attend. We met at the tea house and sat together in one of the larger booths while we waited for our taxi to arrive.

At one point the phone rang and Mrs Lim came and told Shun Yuan it was for him. This really caught me by surprise. I had created a mental image of Shun Yuan floating through the world but not really belonging to it and the fact that somebody could reach him on the telephone forced me once again to reassess my notions.

He came back with a troubled look on his face, made a very rushed apology for not being able to join us and was gone, leaving me looking at the others in the hopes that they had picked something up that I had missed, but getting only shrugs and shakes of the head in return.

The taxi arrived then and we were off to dinner. When we arrived at the restaurant, the owner met Mr Lim and spoke very quickly to him in Taiwanese. I couldn't make anything of it but his body language appeared very apologetic.

After a few moments, Mrs Lim explained to me that the restaurant had overbooked itself and that we would be sharing the grand hall which Mr Lim had booked with two other small groups. Nobody seemed to mind and we went in and sat down at one of the many large round tables, all but the two nearest the door being booked for our dinner party.

In Chinese there is a phrase for a bustling excited energy, which translated literally means "hot noise" and in Taiwan, having a fun dinner out with all your friends is always noisy.

This dinner was no exception and in no time at all, our large group had more than caught up with the two small groups who were there before us.

I do not drink any alcohol, but it seemed that everyone else must do as countless bottles of beer and liquor of various kinds appeared on the tables.

The food was amazing. The restaurant had provided both vegetarian and non-vegetarian choices and I had to really pace myself as round after round of empty dishes were cleared away, to be replaced by more. I particularly liked a certain vegetable dish and was surprised at how quickly this arrived at the table when I had requested another serving.

As the evening drew on, the unmistakable sound of Taiwanese drinking games started to come from one table then the next. Master Hong was sitting to my right and challenged me to a counting game, his face already beetroot red from the alcohol he had drunk. He grudgingly allowed me to stick with cola and despite his obvious inebriation, proceeded to thrash me at the game.

Every time I lost I was to drink whatever cola was left in my glass and it wasn't long before I was ready to burst and had to excuse myself to go to the toilet.

I wandered out through the noisy hall and down the passageway to find the toilet and gave a long satisfied sigh as I relieved myself.

It was a shame that Shun Yuan hadn't been able to make it, but I had really enjoyed the food and the outing was obviously a great success.

I walked back to the grand hall and stood there just inside the doorway, momentarily disoriented and looked around to try and pick out our table, when a glass flew past my face not more than two inches away and I heard it smash over to my right.

All around me the world erupted into chaos and violence. The tone of the general noise and hubbub instantly and completely changed as angry shouts accompanied smashing glass and the sound of tables and chairs being overturned.

I stood there completely at ease and unmoving, not panicked and frozen to the spot, just calm and quiet as I observed fists and feet flying here and there in a hurricane of punches of kicks.

I felt completely sure of my safety as I stood there; knowing that I would respond instantaneously and with whatever movement was required.

Two young men flew past on my right as they fought each other, one landing a punch on the other with a strange thudding sound that I thought sounded nothing at all like punches in the movies. As I watched them they both fell to the floor wrestling.

A blur of motion to my left resolved into the head of another young man, which struck against the door frame beside me with a loud crack and I watched dispassionately as he crumpled straight down onto the floor by my feet.

Then it was over. As quickly as the fight had started it had been broken up and the two groups who had been sitting by the door had been ejected. It never crossed my mind who had ejected them or how anyone had come past me, standing in the doorway as I was.

I walked across to our table, picking my way to avoid stepping on larger pieces of broken glass and as I approached I could see my friends staring at me with a familiar look on their faces. I had always thought of myself as gawping like an idiot when that expression crossed my face, but looking at it now I could see it was pure astonishment.

Mr Lim opened his mouth to say "What" and I cut him off immediately with a gesture.
"Please don't ask me what, or how, or anything about that just now" I said. "I have absolutely no idea what is going on and just want to go home please."

Master Hong was nodding and quietly asking the others to give me some space for a moment. He whispered quiet apologies to me and I understood from him that everyone had been completely shocked by this outburst of violence which was extremely uncommon in Taiwan.

I sat there staring at my empty glass and wondering if this was how Shun Yuan felt when someone asked him how he had accomplished something they had seen him do.

I looked at Master Hong then and asked, "What is he doing to me?" and he replied, "Is this everyday life enough for you Rob?"

I sat there for a few moments more, wondering at my own lack of reaction. I remained completely unruffled by the event and was soon satisfied that a delayed shock reaction was not coming. It was as if I really had been watching a movie, on a giant wraparound screen.

Master Hong and I left together then and took a taxi back to his house, where we sat together and Wayne prepared the most delicious cup of coffee I had ever had.

As I spoke with Wayne that evening I was again struck by the difference in him; he had very clearly chosen the shape he wanted to be and his focused intent was quickly bringing it about.

It was very late when Shun Yuan arrived and he looked completely exhausted. I wondered where he had been, why he had not been able to join us, to share in and witness the events of the evening.

Looking at him then I understood that he had a life which did not entirely revolve around me and I did not question him.

He dropped heavily into the chair next to mine and listened as I told him what had happened. As I was speaking I had a further realization and said, "Stillness. Stillness was absolutely appropriate for the moment. But it's not like I deliberately chose to be still, it's like a great big moving jigsaw puzzle and by being still, I fit so perfectly into the space that it was just as if I was not there."

He told me then, "Some years ago I witnessed one of the greatest expressions of mastery I have ever seen, perhaps that I am ever likely to see. BB King and Ray Charles were playing together here in Taiwan. The music was incredible and as I watched how beautifully relaxed BB King was I knew I was in the presence of a great Master.

It was as if he didn't need his guitar or any accompaniment. As huge as he is, he almost seemed to disappear entirely. He seemed to me like he was simply an opportunity, a channel through which the music just flowed out and into all of us.

I could see the music pouring out of him like a thick golden braid and saw it split into a thousand strands. I could feel it as one strand hit me in the chest and wrapped itself around my core and I felt myself vibrating in harmony with every note that he sang or played. That experience changed me forever."

I was smiling and shaking my head gently and he knew that I had been expecting a tale of martial arts heroics, fit for Master Hong's soap opera.

Then he was smiling at me, that big warm smile of his and said, "It's a very long day tomorrow Rob, try to get some sleep" and with that he closed his eyes and fell asleep right there and then.

I did not sleep at all that night. I sat there in the company of my teacher and thought back through the lessons he had taught me.

Something deep was changing in me, although I still couldn't get to grips with what it was. I did not have the obvious clarity of vision which Wayne was now displaying in his drive to achieve his transmutation.

I drifted back mentally to the breakfast place and once again watched Wayne leaving alone and was very happy that he had indeed found a Master who could see the possibility of gold underneath his leaden exterior.

I looked at Shun Yuan, fast asleep in his chair and wondered where it would lead me, this way of his, which sometimes felt to me as if it was 'the way of the last minute fluke'.

I thought about luck then and came to the conclusion that having completely mastered the state of beginner's mind, Shun Yuan was blessed with an oversized portion of beginner's luck.

Chapter fourteen.

The ninth method.

A great black crow.

A few hours later Shun Yuan stirred. Watching him rouse himself I was reminded of my family cat as he gave a huge stretch in his chair, which included opening his mouth as wide as it would go in a vast yawn. Then he dropped to his knees on the floor and I watched quietly, not wanting to disturb his morning prayer routine.

He gestured that I should join him on the floor and rather than praying as I had expected, took me through more cat-like stretches which had me arching my back and drawing in my stomach as far as I could.

We stood then and went through a series of exercises which Shun Yuan referred to as "Welcoming the Dawn" and told me would prepare my body for the day ahead.

We started off massaging and rubbing our heads with our fingertips until I could feel a gentle buzzing in my scalp. Then we clenched and stretched our facial muscles and anyone looking in the window at that moment would have thought we were completely insane or perhaps competing for the world's ugliest face competition.

After this we performed movements which felt somewhat more normal to me, gently loosening up the whole body from the neck down, starting at each joint with gentle slow movements which we gradually increased in speed.

At the conclusion of the sequence, Shun Yuan had me do an exercise called "nail rasping", which literally meant vigorously rasping the fingernails of my two hands against each other. We did this for a full ten minutes and when we were ready to stop, he had me very slowly open up my hands from their semi-clenched position and gradually stretch them into the expansive open hand posture that I used when doing my circle walking.

The sensation was intense and very pleasurable. It felt something like "pins and needles" but without any of the attendant mild discomfort that I associate with that.

"We work both ways at once Rob" he said while I stood enjoying the feeling in my hands, "from the core outwards and from the edge inwards. Look how engrossed you are in your hands now, almost like a baby who has just discovered he has hands! Remember shortly after I first met you and I told you that you were too much in your head? This is what I was getting at. You are really IN your hands now."

I was nodding my understanding even as I heard myself internally asking why he hadn't just shown me nail rasping back then and replying that I probably wouldn't have understood the point anyway.

The sensation started to fade and I when I mentioned this to Shun Yuan he nodded and said, "Over the course of the day you'll forget you even have hands. Tomorrow morning you can remind yourself again with this exercise. Try to rediscover yourself at every opportunity Rob, whether physically, emotionally or intellectually in small ways or large. You will be rewarded with a profound sense of wonder at what you find."

We went outside then and after observing my circling for a while, Shun Yuan showed me a simple sequence of movements which resulted in me changing direction.

I had gone clockwise up until now, with my right hand extended to the centre of the circle. Going anti-clockwise was another new learning experience, although not as difficult as learning from scratch.

My left arm complained hugely at being held in the correct posture though and I tried to remember if I had had such difficulty with the right one.

I asked Shun Yuan how much time I should spend going each way and he said, "Your left side will soon catch up with your right, so do half and half, but do at least one hundred cycles in one direction before changing to the other."

I looked over to where Wayne and Master Hong had come out and started their own exercises. Shun Yuan explained that Wayne had now begun learning the "Five Element Fists" and that the chopping motion he was currently working on was the first of the five and related to metal.

"Metal is the first element to learn and the last one to master" he said, adding "but Wayne is really doing incredibly well."

After we had spent some time working on our exercises Master Hong called a stop for breakfast. He served us up huge bowls of do-jiang and a kind of seed bread which he baked himself and which had filled the house with a wonderful rich smell.

As we were eating I recalled Shun Yuan's comment the night before, that this would be a long day and asked "What's the plan for the rest of the day then?"

"You have study and work to get on with and I have somewhere I have to be until later this evening, when we will meet at the tea house. Mrs Lim is making a donation tonight at an initiation ceremony where some lay folk are taking up robes to become monks of their Order. Mrs Lim's nephew will be among them, he's joining for the next year as I understand it."

"I'm not sure I'm invited" I said. I didn't recall Mrs Lim having mentioned anything about the event and didn't want to gate-crash.

"Of course you're invited" Shun Yuan replied, "It's the whole family, even Sofia will be there, she's come up by train to attend."

I felt really strange then. I did continue to feel a bond with Mrs Lim and her family, but did I feel that I was actually part of it? I decided it couldn't hurt to go along with being the latest adopted member.

Just then I had a flashback to the events of the night before and assured myself that however crowded, I was unlikely to see drunken violence at a religious initiation.

Once we had finished breakfast I made use of Master Hong's shower, instantly regretting the decision as I discovered the water was freezing cold. I gritted my teeth hard and stayed in as long as I could, before leaping out and shivering wildly, my teeth chattering all the while I dried and dressed myself.

I couldn't remember the last time I had been that cold and although this might be a moment that Shun Yuan would call a rediscovery, I thought to myself that there must be others which did not involve getting quite so close to hypothermia.

The cold had served one purpose; I was really wide awake despite not having slept. A quickly guzzled cup of Wayne's spectacular coffee further energized me and I had to remind myself to slow down several times on the drive back to the tea house.

When I arrived Mrs Lim was anxious to know how I was doing and I could tell that she was feeling guilty about the night before. I told her I was absolutely fine and that there was no way she or her brother could possibly have foreseen what had happened. I hadn't taken a scratch and that was all that mattered. I told her then that Shun Yuan had mentioned the ceremony which was to be held later and admitted that I couldn't recall if she had told me before. I also said that I felt I didn't deserve to be treated by her as well as she did.

She laughed this off and thanked me for coming and then caught me completely off guard by giving me a warm hug. That dissolved any remaining hesitance I might have had about my adoption and I looked anew at her.
"Call me auntie" she said, tousling my hair as if I was a little child.
"Auntie" I replied, "I have a lot to get through before tonight so please excuse me now" and I went up to my room to get my things together and go off about my day.

The time flew by. Despite working as quickly as I could, it was early evening before I had returned to the tea house and flung my things into my cupboard.

When I went downstairs Mrs Lim told me that Sofia was not going to make it because of a problem with her train. To my concerned look she reassured me that there had been no accident, just a technical hiccup which had left Sofia down in Kaohsiung. Then she told me that Shun Yuan was sitting in a booth by the door and I walked over to see him.

It was an odd sensation, walking up to his booth again and seeing him sitting there, this time reading a book. Just as he had before, without looking up from the page he raised his arm and a single extended finger indicated to me that I should wait while he finished what he was doing.

I reached down and grabbed at his finger and he twisted his arm and grabbed my sleeve, pulling down on it sharply. This caused me to topple forwards onto my knees and my dignity was further thrashed by Morning walking past behind me at that very moment and letting out a loud snort of a

176

laugh.

"What have you done for her?" Shun Yuan asked and to my shame I had to admit that I had forgotten completely about it. His shaking head and pursed lips were more than enough chastisement and I promised to work something out within the week.

Trying to change the subject I mentioned that while reading that day I had come across reference to a monk known as "Hangzhou Tianlong", meaning the Heavenly Dragon of Hangzhou. He was apparently famous for using a single raised finger to answer the questions of his disciples and I wondered if there was any relation to Shun Yuan's Heavenly Dragon.

Shun Yuan shook his head, "No, there is no relation, just the coincidence of a shared name" he said, "and you should be glad of that Rob."

"Why's that?" I asked.

"Because that Master is famous for having helped one of his disciples achieve enlightenment by chopping off his finger!" I hadn't come across this while reading and to the worried look on my face, Shun Yuan's expression in response became an evil grin.

"In the end Rob" he said, "You'll have to lop off a lot more than a finger."

"It doesn't feel like stuff is getting lopped off" I said.

"I mean you've given me so much already." Shun Yuan then told me that everything I had learned, all the exercises, were tools to whittle away at myself.

"Until I bring out the perfect shape" I said.

To that he replied by telling me the story of a Master mason, who had been asked to create a perfectly round stone ball to adorn the court of a nobleman. The mason began by chipping at a huge block until he had created the basic shape of the sphere, then began gradually working with finer and finer tools until he was polishing the ball with his finest polishing cloth.

He called for the nobleman to come and inspect his work and the nobleman asked his little daughter to run her fingers over the surface of the sphere. She complained that it was still rough, so the mason went on polishing.

When he thought it was ready he called for the nobleman again. Once again he brought his daughter and she complained that the ball was still too rough.

Determined that his work would not be rejected a third time, the mason worked day and night on the ball, losing himself completely in his work.

When finally the nobleman's daughter, now grown into a woman, came one day to tell the mason that her father had died, she found him sitting on the dusty floor of his empty workshop with a smile on his face.

He asked the noblewoman if the ball were now smooth enough and she agreed that it was and paid him his fee.

Little Rabbit turned up just then with some food and we sat enjoying our dinner together, Shun Yuan making little noises of delight now and again and reminding me of a little baby as he smacked his lips and grinned to himself.

I knew there were a ton of things I had intended to ask him, that my journal was full of questions to be posed or clarifications requested, but I just sat there enjoying his company and the food until Mrs Lim came to tell us it was time to get going.

We went outside to where Mrs Lim's car was parked and a huge suitcase stood next to it. I stood looking at the suitcase for a long time, as if perhaps by the intensity of my stare I could shrink it down a bit. There was no way it was going to fit in Mrs Lim's car. I wasn't even sure that the three of us would fit.

In the end Shun Yuan and I heaved it onto the roof and tied it in place, needing to leave the windows slightly open and pass the ropes through them because the car had no roof-rack. The car sunk into whatever little suspension it had with the weight of the suitcase and I thought there was no way it could possibly take us all as well. I clambered into the back, which seemed to have been designed for carrying Mrs Lim's handbag.

"How long is the drive?" I asked, wondering if I would be able to straighten myself up again after doing the journey curled up in the foetal position. Mrs Lim misunderstood me and said that we had plenty of time to get there before she had to present her donation. With Shun Yuan and Mrs Lim now in the front seats I felt the little car straining even more.

We set off then, Mrs Lim making a comment that I only half understood, something about the steering which left me worried again at the ability of the vehicle to get us to our destination.

Crunched up as I was I couldn't see anything out of the window and I was opening my mouth to try and start a conversation to take my mind off my discomfort when we hit a vicious pot-hole and I felt something in my side pull.

I let out a little gasp and when Shun Yuan asked if I was alright I did the polite thing and said I was fine, all the while cursing myself for not having slept the night before as he had suggested.

After what felt like hours I mentioned that it didn't feel like we were moving very fast and Mrs Lim told me that the traffic was particularly bad, but that we still had enough time to reach the ceremony on time.

Eventually we escaped the traffic jam and began making better time, which I could tell by the frequency with which we went over pot-holes and I had to clench down on my need to squeak in discomfort. The time dragged on and I could feel the pain in my side slowly getting worse until I thought I couldn't take it any longer and would have to ask Mrs Lim to stop.

"We're here" said Shun Yuan and I silently thanked all the gods as the car came to a halt.

It took me a long time to get out of the car and as I tried to straighten myself I felt a strong twinge of pain down the left hand side of my back. Shun Yuan noticed me wincing and I admitted that I had hurt my back. Mrs Lim looked worriedly at me and I tried to assure her that I would be ok, but my back had started to spasm and I winced at every twitch which seemed to alarm her greatly.

While Mrs Lim applied her hands to my back, which gave a very small bit of relief, Shun Yuan untied the ropes and slid the suitcase off the roof of the car. It thumped loudly on the ground as it landed.

I looked around, not knowing where I was and unable to make out much in the dim light.

"Point me in the right direction" I said, to which Shun Yuan pointed at the sky with his finger. I thought he was making a joke or a reference to the monk we had talked about earlier, but as I peered over at him I realized that we were parked at the bottom of a long flight of steps that ran very steep up the side of a hill.

"No way" I said gesturing towards the suitcase, "I might just about drag myself up there by the end of the night, but there's no way we are getting that thing up there. I'm afraid my back is done for and unless there is someone else here to help" I left the rest of the thought unspoken, completing my meaning with a shrug and a look around. Shun Yuan walked over to the suitcase and said "Everyone else will be inside already." Then he told Mrs Lim "Take care of the cripple" and with that he hefted the case up against his chest and raced up the stairs, disappearing into the deepening dark.

I was just thinking to myself "no way", when Mrs Lim gave a little cry of surprise.

"Oh, it's like a great black crow has flown off with my baggage" she said. As she helped me up the stairs I was left to ponder the weight of my own baggage and to what extent I continued to be limited by the preconceptions I carried around in my head.

We got to the top of the stairs, which didn't take as long as I had feared it might, but was a very difficult climb nonetheless; every step I climbed eliciting a new twinge of pain. I looked around for Shun Yuan and spotted him standing at the doorway of a building, the suitcase being carried inside by two other people. He was gesturing as if to say "come on slow-pokes" and I could only laugh, which made my side hurt like hell.

We were indeed the last to arrive and even as I gingerly knelt down on the bright orange cushion provided for me the ceremony had begun.

This was a noisy affair, with trumpets blown and bells rung and incantations which it seemed to me were shouted as opposed to chanted.

The noise was only outdone by the colour scheme which was wild. The walls of the hall were red and a mass of multi-coloured pennants hung, each one bearing a different symbol, which I did not recognize and which Mrs Lim whispered were magical wards.

A large golden Buddha statue sat in the centre of the far wall and surrounding him were countless figurines of deities which reminded me of Master Hong's shrine.

A ledge ran around the edge of the room at about shoulder height and held dozens of tiny brass dishes which contained wicks burning in scented oil.

The monks of this Order wore a reddish coloured robe and had yellow hats. The only similar thing I had seen was pictures of Tibetan monks and although the décor of the place was also highly reminiscent, I did not recognize anything that I saw as being specifically Tibetan.

The new initiates, barely visible through thick clouds of incense smoke, prostrated themselves in front of the Buddha as the Master spoke incantations and wove his hands in a continuous series of mudras.

The whole thing would have been completely fascinating if I could have ignored the pain in my back, which was now constant and causing me to clench my hands and teeth and squeeze my eyes shut in an effort to master it.

When the ceremony ended I was unable to get up without Shun Yuan's help and he led me to a side room and laid me down on the floor.

One of the monks came in and offered to help with some massage and I groaned as he rolled me onto my stomach. He probed and prodded different spots on my back, telling me that this was his method of diagnosis and causing me to moan in pain each time one his knuckles hit a particular area.

"This is going to be quite energetic" he said, "please prepare yourself" and as I winced with the expectation of pain he laid his palm on my back and made a sudden movement. There was no flash of new pain, in fact the relief was immediate and caused me to laugh out loud.

I thanked the monk for his massage and Shun Yuan reached a hand out to me to help me up saying, "I'll bet you've forgotten that you have hands but you are more aware than ever of your back."

I accepted his help up and said, "I'm not sitting in the back. Why don't you jog home? You can have tea ready

182

for the rest of us when we get there." He laughed at that and I said, "Honestly how the hell did you get that thing up the stairs?"

"It didn't come for free Rob" he replied. I pushed him for more of an explanation and he said then, "Do you remember what happened with Gareth that second time?"

"When you almost broke his leg?" I asked.

"There was no danger of that" he said, "but yes, that's the time. Tonight was something like that. It's a bit like taking all the energy that you might expend doing your circling during one whole session and coiling it all up and letting it all go at once."

"How do you do that?" I went on and he replied only, "By deciding to."

All the way back as I rode in the front with Mrs Lim, I found myself thinking about his simple statement. Even as I struggled with the idea I found myself thinking about the changes that I had made in myself by deciding to do so, about the radical changes I saw in Wayne which were clearly a result of his decision to reshape his life.

When we arrived I got out and stood at the side of the alley to watch while Shun Yuan poured out of the back of the car as if he was made of honey. Then as he straightened up he did a weird twisting movement which spiralled through his body and made him look like he was possessed by the spirit of a snake, leaving me wondering where Mrs Lim's crow or the cat of earlier that morning had gone.

Chapter fifteen.

The tenth method.

The crash.

"There is somebody that I'd like you to meet" said Shun Yuan one afternoon as we sat in the tea house drinking tea and eating Mrs Lim's excellent shui-jao dumplings.
"It's a long way though and I'm not sure if your scooter will make it" he added. I looked at him wondering how he was going to make it and seeing the question on my face he said, "Oh Master Hong will loan me a scooter, he owns a repair shop in town and one of his lads will be able to spare one for a while."
"How come Master Hong's scooter will make it if mine won't?" I asked, to which he grinned and whispered something about certain modifications that Master Hong's lads tended to make to their vehicles.

As it happened, the next morning when Master Hong heard of the trip Shun Yuan was planning, he said that my scooter should have no problems, but that if it died going up one of the hills and we got stranded in the middle of nowhere we could always call him.

This didn't exactly fill me with confidence, as small as it is Taiwan has some pretty severe terrain, particularly when you are driving a scooter designed for the city, but I left aside concerns such as finding a telephone in the middle of nowhere and the length of time we might have to wait before being rescued.

We planned the trip for one Saturday a few weeks away, Shun Yuan apparently wanting to give plenty of notice of our arrival before we showed up.

Morning was on my mind all the time. I was struggling hugely with finding a way to thank her without it being obvious it was from me. Time and again I found myself walking up to Mrs Lim to ask what I could do for her, only to stop and turn around, telling myself that this was something I had to figure out on my own. I realized that my difficulty was largely due to the fact that I knew almost nothing about her and cursed myself for not having taken the opportunity to get to know her better before upsetting her so.

I took to eavesdropping on her conversations with Swift and Little Rabbit and it was one of these that eventually provided me with my chance. The girls were sitting in the staff area eating dinner one evening when I heard Morning's voice raised in excitement, caused I learned by the imminent arrival of a pop star from Hong Kong, the latest heartthrob to have captured the attention of half of Taiwan's population of young women.

I paused for a few moments thinking about the three of them as young women. I had mistakenly guessed them all as several years younger than they really were.

It was easy enough to get tickets for the concert and Mrs Lim readily agreed to let Morning have the evening off when I finally approached her with the idea. She even agreed to give Morning the tickets, with a made up story that they were a gift from some other customer who had been passing through. That was about the best I could come up with. I would just have to hope that the other girls were not too put out by having to cover Morning's shift.

I was in my room when a scream of delight coming from below told me that Mrs Lim had presented Morning with the envelope containing the tickets. I wasn't sure if it was enough, but I nodded to myself thinking "It will do."

It was ten days later when Morning walked up to me and

said "Idiot" without any venom in her voice. I shrugged my shoulders and said "I know" and when she walked off I felt that we had perhaps reached some kind of truce, although I wished she had not seen through my ruse quite so easily.

One afternoon when I arrived at Master Hong's I found Wayne practising a movement sequence which he told me was based on a combination of all the Chinese elements; Metal, Water, Wood, Fire and Earth. He had also begun learning forms based on animals he said and proceeded to demonstrate a Chicken form.

I couldn't help sniggering internally when he mentioned the name, but as he went through his demonstration I quickly took back any association I had with cowardice. I've never seen a cock-fight but have heard them described as brutal affairs and watching his form I thought that this Chicken must be based on observation of the creatures fighting for territory or mates in the wild. His arms became wings which buffeted and battered his imaginary opponent while his fingers made the shape of the bird's beak and attacked vital areas such as the eyes and throat.

Yet again Wayne had surprised me with the degree of his transformation and when I mentioned this to him he said, "It's all thanks to my Master. I was so lost before; really I had no idea what I was doing. When I first met you and Shun Yuan in the park, I had become so attached to what I had been doing and so arrogant about it. Looking back now it was just stupid. If Shun Yuan hadn't woken me up and then introduced me to Master Hong, I'd still be doing empty rubbish and boasting about it. Without that introduction I don't think there's any way that Master Hong would have accepted me as a student, even if I had been able to find him. Now I'm living here with him as his disciple! Do you find it difficult knowing that Shun Yuan could move on at any time? Are you planning on going with him?"

Wayne's questions caught me by surprise. I realized that I had assumed that Shun Yuan had decided to stay where he was long term and once again this assumption had simply come out of my mind without anything to base it on.

"I really have no idea" I replied.

"Our relationship certainly doesn't have the formality that you have with Master Hong. I do think of him as my teacher and when I called him that he didn't object, but I haven't spoken to him about it and I should have. I'm really enjoying what I'm learning and I know I have a long way to go."

That evening I asked Shun Yuan how long he intended to stay at Master Hong's.

"As long as he'll have me" he replied and then, "There's something you need to understand Rob. I am here at the moment because the tide brought me back here. That's the best way I can explain it. When it is time to go, the tide will turn and I will ride it off to whatever new place it takes me to."

"Can't you drop anchor for a while? Just decide to stay?" I asked.

"I don't have such an anchor, not at the moment anyway" he replied.

"Perhaps one day such a thing will be possible, but I want to be open with you and say that right now, when the tide turns I will move on."

I thought about that for a long while before asking "Are you able to steer? I mean do you just find yourself washed up somewhere or can you tack across the current and choose where to go, even if you can't stay put?"

"I am an extremely poor navigator" he said grinning.

"I tried a few times, to see if I could bend the forces which move me to my own will. The results were disastrous. It simply wasn't the right time and I was hopelessly unprepared. I've learned a lot by the experience though and for now I am content to go where the current goes."

"Did I tell you that I dreamed about you surfing?" I asked and thinking about the way that he seemed rooted to the ground I added "I bet you would be amazing at that."

Master Hong erupted with a huge laugh at that and spilled half the soup from the noodles he was carrying over to us from the kitchen.

"Shun Yuan on a surfboard?! That'll be the day!" he roared. "He can't even stay upright on a skateboard!"

"It's true" Shun Yuan nodded. "The local kids here have tried countless times to teach me without success. My centre objects to the way the board wants to move and tends to stubbornly stay where it is, which usually means that I fall flat on my ass as soon as I stand on the thing."

I thought back to the incident in the park with the young man, where Shun Yuan's body had pivoted around his centre which somehow had remained fixed where it was in space, despite his feet being up in the air.

"You know what?" I said, "I don't think that's too much of a price to pay for what you have gained. So you'll never impress the girls down at the skate rink with your skills. The way you dress they are hardly going to be queuing up for attention anyway!"

He looked down at his robes and appeared to be pondering my statement for a while.

"So it's the robes that put them off then?" he asked.

"I had wondered." He was completely straight faced and for the life of me I couldn't tell if he was joking so I asked, "Aren't you celibate? I thought all monks took a vow when they put on robes."

He was shaking his head before I had finished.

"No, not at all. There are many Orders which are celibate it's true, however it would be wrong to assume that all Orders include such vows. My Order only requires a vow of celibacy from monks who are more senior than I am. If I wish to progress to the next Circle, custom dictates that I would have to take such a vow."

"What's the next circle?" I asked.

"The way in which our hierarchy is organized is as a series of concentric circles" he explained, drawing circles in the air with his finger.

"There are several outer rings of lay people, several rings for those who have committed to the Order for a limited period of time and then more for those of us who intend to be lifelong Adepts. There is a possibility of the centre of the circle representing a monastery or some fixed place around which the rest is laid out, but the Order hasn't had such a place for a long time. It's just a shame that many of the rings are so sparsely populated these days, but in an Order with a largely oral tradition and no fixed centre, it can be very difficult to recruit new blood."

"I hadn't realized that the circle played such an important part" I said. "I really hadn't thought about it as part of your iconography."

"It's critical" Shun Yuan replied. "In fact some of our most important lessons are conveyed by the image of a circle, not to mention the physical exercises you are working on."

With that he asked Master Hong for some paper, a brush and ink and drew a symbol; a circle with a dot in the centre. "Here" he said, handing me the sheet when it had dried, "this will keep you busy for a while."

"What do I do with it?" I asked, looking at the paper and feeling as if it looked back at me with its single unblinking eye.

"You might start by looking at it and go on with thinking about it. Think about what it represents, other than the hierarchy of my Order that is!" He reached into his robe for something.

"This thing is given to all our novices to contemplate" he explained. "I'm still carrying the one I was given, although it has seen better days" and with that he withdrew a folded piece of paper with the same mark on it, but clearly made by a different hand.

Looking at the paper he said, "One day I might even improve my brushwork enough that I can draw them as beautifully as this. Just like skateboarding, calligraphy is certainly not one of my strong suits."

The Friday evening before our trip soon came and Shun Yuan asked me to stay at Master Hong's that night. It became clear why when he roused me at four in the morning to go through his daily routine of Welcoming the Dawn and then shower and hurriedly eat some breakfast before heading off.

We set out from Taipei and began a long drive, generally South and East through increasingly steep terrain. Shun Yuan's borrowed scooter had no problems with the climbs, but he frequently had to stop to allow me to catch up.

We drove for hours, stopping briefly for fuel or a drink of water and a bite to eat. After a time I found myself once again completely lost and disoriented.

Finally we approached a small town near the coast and just on the other side of this reached our destination; a large house surrounded by a high wall which was surmounted by red tiles.

We parked the scooters in an alley along one side of the wall and Shun Yuan led me through a gate and into a garden, where I could see someone practising what I thought were the circling movements of Bagua. A few moments observation however and I had to correct myself. These were not the same movements that I saw Shun Yuan practising or that he had taught me so far.

"That isn't your Bagua is it? I remember a while ago you telling me that I wouldn't be able to tell the difference between your Bagua and the circling done by other members of your Order!" I beamed a smile at him, happy to be able to demonstrate in some small way that I had learned something at least. He looked at me and smiled in return.

"Well, we still don't know if you can tell the difference or not Rob" he said. "This gentleman is learning Bagua from the man who owns this house, Master Liu. When I first came here years ago, Master Liu was kind enough to teach me until he could arrange for an introduction to the person who became my Master."

"But other than the circling, it doesn't look anything like the Bagua that you practise or that you are teaching me. In fact even the circling looks a bit different" I said confused.

"It feels very different too, that's why I'm not still doing this method today" he replied. "Master Liu realized that I just wasn't suited to it so he introduced me to one of his friends" he went on.

"Bagua is an art form that is spread across a big family tree. The founder of what we call Bagua today had many students and each one of them had a different background and came away with a different understanding, creating different branches of the art. The same has happened at each new generation, so some of the modern day forms are very closely related to my practice and others are more like distant cousins. There are plenty that I've never even met!"

Just then a man came out of the house into the garden and

Shun Yuan broke into a huge smile and cried out "Master Liu!"

Despite my continued inability to judge the age of Chinese people with any degree of accuracy, it was obvious that Master Liu was old. He was I thought, probably the only person I had seen who looked to be clearly older than Old Li that I had met in the park in Taipei, yet for all that, he moved much more fluidly.

"Look at him" said Shun Yuan still smiling, "This is the result of a lifetime of practice."

Master Liu was calling back in reply, "It is a strange thing when stray cats wander in to my garden from the street and call me Master!"

Shun Yuan grinned an even bigger smile and said, "Perhaps you haven't been listening, but I hear that every evening they sit on the wall and serenade you in thanks for the beauty of your form!"

Shun Yuan bowed a deep bow and the two men shook hands, then he introduced me as his student. Master Liu shook my hand and I was surprised that his hands, which were thick and large and looked extremely strong, were also very soft and did not deliver the crushing handshake I had been half expecting.

"Why so long?" Master Liu asked of Shun Yuan.

"I know, I know. We would have come before, but your students told me how busy you had been. Congratulations on the birth, how many grandchildren is it now?"

Master Liu beamed a smile and proudly announced that he now had seventeen grandchildren and four great grandchildren. He pointed out the gentleman who was still circling in the garden and announced that he was grandchild number one.

"I wondered if perhaps you could give Rob here a taste of your form" ventured Shun Yuan, with a deference that I had not seen in him before.

"It's all very well him watching me, but from you he will get an idea of what's really achievable."

Master Liu gestured to us to take a seat on a wooden bench that stood over to one side and without saying a word began performing his version of the form. When I'd seen him walking out of the house I had thought that he moved better than Old Li, but as I watched I was transfixed by how effortlessly he performed movements which by then I knew from experience would have left me heaving for breath on the floor.

As I watched closely I could see that this form was indeed a more distant relation to the one that Shun Yuan practised. Master Liu's form went from circling, which tended to be very small circles or even spinning on the spot, to suddenly branch out in wide sweeps and although some of the movements held a certain similarity, for the most part I didn't recognize anything of what he did.

I let out a small hoot of surprise when at one point Master Liu leapt into the air. This was completely unexpected, both because I had never seen Shun Yuan do anything of the sort and of course because I was watching a man who could easily be in his late nineties or older leaping about like he was thirty.

When he had finished, Shun Yuan gave him a hearty round of applause and Master Liu bowed and said, "No, you are too kind" over and over.

Master Liu then asked to see my circling and I very nervously agreed and did my best to make a good circle and demonstrate the method I had been shown for changing direction. Master Liu nodded at me in what I hoped was approval and then asked me what else I was learning. The tui-shou I had been doing with Peng came immediately to mind and a moment later I found myself with the old Master standing in front of me, ready to practise together.

I couldn't help starting extremely cautiously, as if something in me was still worried that Master Liu was made of glass and fearful that I would break him. I was still carrying around the remnants of my beliefs concerning the abilities of people as they got older and when I realized this I put some more effort into the exercise.

Pushing with him was an odd thing. He was nothing at all like Peng or even Shun Yuan. While Peng would have shaken me to pieces and Shun Yuan would have evaporated and left me pushing at the air, Master Liu somehow made me feel continually off-balance so that I was never able to really apply any force towards him.

Every now and again, just at the perfect moment when my balance was at greatest danger of toppling, he gave me a tiny nudge which sent me stumbling off to one side. I noticed that I could spot when he was setting me up for a move which would unbalance me, but always just that bit too late so that it was almost as if my realization of the precariousness of my situation was part of the ammunition he was using to defeat me.

It was just then that I thought that this was just like chess and once again cursed myself for not having paid more attention to that first lesson that Shun Yuan had tried to share and doubly for not yet having asked him to repeat it.

We practised together for a short while longer and then Master Liu invited us indoors. To my backward glance at his grandson, Master Liu replied that he would be busy circling for quite some time and ushered me in.

We sat in an immaculately clean room. The walls were painted a bright almost ivory white and were hung with portraits, some of which depicted people whom I thought could have lived hundreds of years ago by their dress.

Master Liu pointed to each one in turn and rattled off a name, telling me that they were all Masters of Bagua.

As I looked around I saw polished wooden chairs that lined the walls most of the way around. The centre of the room was dominated by a beautiful circular table, about the same size as Master Hong's table but clearly antique; the central column on which it stood carved with intertwined dragons.

At one end was a large shrine with many figurines of deities, but devoid of the piles of incense ash that covered Master Hong's shrine. Instead three bowls contained offerings; one of water, one of uncooked rice and one with a single coin in it.

A woman who Master Liu introduced as his eldest granddaughter came in a moment later with tea and we all sat and enjoyed this together.

We eventually bid our farewells, Mr Liu giving me his name card and asking me to call or stop by if I needed anything. When we were in the alleyway, Shun Yuan looked at me and said, "Ninety six. I just hope that I have a fraction of what he has when I am that old." I could only nod in agreement and thought back on the demonstration he had given us which, considering his age, left me dumbfounded.

It was already getting quite dark so I breathed a sigh of relief to myself when we reached a road that I recognized as being on the outskirts of Taipei. We had spent almost the entire day on the road getting to Master Liu's and back and although I had loved every minute of our visit, I was getting very tired and wanted to be off the scooter and in my bed.

As we approached a junction a noise in front startled me. I looked ahead and to my right where Shun Yuan was driving and my perception of the world went into slow motion and snapped into incredible detail, despite the darkness.

A cable which must have somehow come loose and hung down across the road had caught Shun Yuan around the neck, another loop getting twisted around the handlebars of his scooter. His hands flew up from the handlebars and grabbed the cable. Then somehow his centre flew up so that he was lying horizontally in the air as he pulled at the cable and thrust it away from his throat.

The scooter wobbled wildly and Shun Yuan flew along in the air, still horizontal and landed on his back at the far side of the intersection. The scooter had crashed into the wall just to his side.

I jammed on the brakes as hard as I could, causing my scooter to swerve violently as the wheels locked up, almost throwing me off. I let it fall right there at the side of the road without thought, without any capability of thought. My mind was reeling with panic and I was sick to my stomach and desperately trying not to vomit as I leapt over the falling vehicle and ran as hard as I could across the intersection to where my friend and Master lay unmoving, his own scooter a shattered wreck tangled still in the cable that had brought it down.

He was lying there on his back, at the side of the road where he had landed, just staring at his right hand. When I got to him and he saw me standing over him he turned the palm of his hand towards me.
"Just look at this" he said. "I'll be scarred for life." I peered at his hand but could not make anything out and cursed the fact that the streetlights were not working. Shun Yuan sprang to his feet then, still staring at his palm. His robes were a tattered mess but I could see no sign of serious

injury and he displayed no sign of any other hurt, which I thought was a miracle given that neither of us was wearing any kind of protective clothing or helmets.

A door opened and a gentleman came out and helped me move the wrecked scooter completely out of the way. Shun Yuan stood in the light coming from the doorway looking at the palm of his right hand and poking at it with the forefinger of his left.

I walked over to him and looked at his hand to see the tiniest of abrasions, right at the base of his palm. He looked at it as if it was a mortal wound. I was much more concerned by the bright red line across his throat and stood there wondering how he had come through this with nothing but a scratch and thinking that if I had had the faster scooter, I would probably be lying on the floor decapitated or at the least strangled to death.

I took the address down from the gentleman who had come out to offer help and managed to get my scooter started, then drove the two of us the rest of the way back to Master Hong's.

All the way I could tell that Shun Yuan was looking at his hand and when we arrived, the first words he said to Master Hong on seeing him were, "I'll carry this forever." With that he walked into the house and I was left standing with Master Hong.

"Where's the other scooter?" he asked me with a confused look on his face and I handed him the address I had jotted down.

"I can't explain what has happened" I said, "But I really do think Shun Yuan cheated death tonight and he thinks that little mark on his hand is of some profound significance."

I walked into the house after him and found him sitting in the dining room. In his left hand was a pair of tweezers with which he was picking at some tiny pieces of grit which had become lodged in the scratch.

I gave voice to the decision I had made and said, "Master, it's very late and that crash must have been a real shock. Why don't you get some rest?" He was staring at me from the moment I called him Master and I held his gaze until finally he nodded saying, "Very well then. Go back home and make sure you sleep well."

Chapter sixteen.

The paving slab lesson.

When I arrived back at the tea house I thought there was no way I would possibly sleep, but sleep I did and very deeply at that. I woke up much later than usual in the morning and for the first time in a while I did not recall any of the details of my dreams. I was sure I had dreamed, but each time I tried to bring a memory of the dream to mind it evaded me.

It was too late to go to the park, so after a quick shower and a rummage through my wardrobe for a couple of books which I stuffed in my backpack, I walked down to a café near Mrs Lim's tea house to have my breakfast American style. I sat there and enjoyed a plate of pancakes slathered with butter and syrup and a bottomless cup of coffee and flicked through the books I had brought out.

When the caffeine from the third or fourth coffee kicked in I had an intense flashback to the crash the night before and my hands started shaking uncontrollably. I thought it would be a good idea to go back and check on the scooter to see just how much damage I had done to it and decide whether it needed to go into Master Hong's shop for repair, so after paying I walked back up to the tea house and round the corner of the alleyway where the scooter was parked.

I could tell from a distance that something looked wrong and as I walked closer I could see a large black lump on the seat. When I got right up to it I saw that it was something wrapped up in a black cloth and as I unfolded the cloth I realized that I had a tattered piece of Shun Yuan's robe in my hands. Wrapped inside the bundle was a paving slab broken in two and I had no doubt at all that this was the very slab that I had challenged Shun Yuan to break with an "appropriate" technique and he had cast to the floor as he challenged me to throw away my preconceptions.

Under the pieces of the slab was a thick stack of papers, but when I read the first one I had a tremendous sinking feeling in my stomach and for a moment I thought I was going to pass out. On it in handwritten English across the middle of the page were the words "The tide turned."

I shoved the rest of the papers in my backpack and ran in through the side door of the tea house, grabbing Sofia's helmet from where it hung on a hook inside the door and not caring about the garish pink colour and sparkly stickers which adorned it. I went back out into the alleyway, threw the pieces of the slab off to one side out of the way and jumped on the scooter.

I rode as quickly as I dared, which understandably was pretty slowly, over to Master Hong's house. He was there on the grass with Wayne and as I rode up he waved a hello. I parked and ran over to them and asked if he knew where Shun Yuan was. Master Hong's shaken head replied with the answer I had dreaded to hear.

"He borrowed some clothes and left early this morning." he said. "Although perhaps you know something more and I shouldn't expect to see those clothes again for a while?" he wondered.

I sat down on Master Hong's bench feeling deflated and he and Wayne retreated into the house to give me a minute, my expression obviously speaking volumes where my dry mouth did not.

My mind started to race. He wasn't wearing his robes. Of course not, they were shredded. Had I driven right past him on the way here? Had he been sitting in the very same place where I had eaten breakfast only for me to pass him by without noticing? Should I be trying to find him now?

I decided that I should not and sat there on the bench until my racing mind slowed down. I opened my backpack and took out the papers and looked again at the three words which had rendered me an orphan.

"The tide turned."

I sat and stared at that page for a very long time until Wayne came out with coffee for me.
"I left it too late" I said. "Here you have been this whole time, showing me exactly what I needed to do and I failed to see the lesson right in front of me."
"I had no idea this was what you wanted" Wayne replied.
"I don't think I did either" I said. Wayne turned around and went back into the house and I sat there alone and drank his coffee.

When I had finished I looked at the second sheet of paper in the stack. On it was a poem, four lines handwritten in Chinese characters, in imitation of one of the classical styles I had been studying:

問我怎麼打
不是不肯說
實際上我道
講的不結果

Which I translate as:

You ask me how it's done
It's not that I won't say
In fact this Tao of mine
Just can't be shared that way

I smiled then thinking of him, of how I could never understand how he did the things I had seen, but knowing that being there and experiencing them was far more important to me.

I put the second sheet of paper aside with the first and saw that the rest of the papers were loosely attached together in a sheaf.

The cover sheet, as I took it to be, read "Heavenly Dragon Internal Family. Fundamental exercises."

On the first page inside that Shun Yuan had written a dedication:

'Robert, in the traditional manner I am presenting you with my work. Study it diligently and you will find it deepens the understanding which you have already started to demonstrate and provides for a foundation upon which you can continue to grow, through greatness and one day exceeding the heavens themselves. Shun Yuan.'

I turned through the pages, which were all hand written, the text accompanied by diagrams and illustrations of the body, some depicting static postures, others clearly intended to demonstrate motion. Some of the exercises described were well known to me by now and others were entirely new.

Master Hong came over to me then and sat down.
"You have a lot to work on until you see him again" he said.
"I never asked" I said, "How long was it between his visits to you here?"
"It's usually about five years" he replied. "Are you going to stick around in Taiwan until he shows up again?"
"No" I said, and lifting up the sheaf of papers told him, "I have studies to finish here and then I'm going home to start working on these fundamentals that he has left me. In fact, I think I had better get going and let you get back to your own work. I would like to thank you very much for all your hospitality." Master Hong insisted that I keep visiting regularly and told me to call on him if I ever needed

anything. I glanced over at the scooter and told him that I might be in need of some minor repairs.

I rode the scooter back to Mrs Lim's and when I saw her I told her that Shun Yuan had moved on, then I had the sudden feeling that something was missing and rifling through my backpack I realized that I had not kept the tattered piece of robe in which he had wrapped my gift. As sentimental as it might seem, it was immediately important to me to keep it and I went back out into the alleyway to see if it was still there.

I spotted it immediately; I had flung it off to the side of the alley with the pieces of the paving slab. I walked over and retrieved it and noticed that I had missed another piece of paper which was caught up in a fold of the cloth.

Attached to this with a staple was a business card, the name and address written in simplified Chinese characters which I had difficulty with, but I knew were indicating a place in mainland China.

On the paper in Shun Yuan's hand, were written the words:

'Come on in. The water's fine!'

If you have enjoyed this taste of time spent with the Adept and would like to learn more about the Heavenly Dragon Order, Bagua or any of the other methods described in this book, please contact the author at:

rbrtshffr@gmail.com